1903

The bittersweet coming-of-age of a young girl in a turn-of-the-century farm community.

Ellen, an impulsive, high-spirited girl, loves and hates as only a teenager can. It isn't easy being the oldest girl in a family of ten, but Ellen flirts and dreams after the farm chores are done—until she realizes that another child is on the way to steal what little is left of her privacy. How can she handle the terrifying new feelings that have turned her into a brooding stranger to those she loves the most?

Whether brimming with tears or bursting with humor— each page of NEVER MISS A SUNSET is a moment to treasure, as winter turns to spring and Ellen "comes of age" with wonder and delight.

Never Miss a Sunset

Jeanette Gilge

David C. Cook Publishing Co.
ELGIN, ILLINOIS—WESTON, ONTARIO

NEVER MISS A SUNSET
Copyright © 1975 David C. Cook Publishing Co.
First Printing, June 1975
Second Printing, December 1975
Third Printing, June 1976
Fourth Printing, December 1976
Fifth Printing, June 1977
Sixth Printing, December 1977
Seventh Printing, April 1978
Eighth Printing, December 1978
Ninth Printing, February 1979
Tenth Printing, September 1979
Eleventh Printing, March 1980

David C. Cook Publishing Co., Elgin, IL 60120

Printed in the United States of America
Library of Congress Catalog Number: 74-29050
ISBN: 0-912692-56-1

To the memory of my Aunt Ella Rhody,
who told me the story
upon which this book is based.

ACKNOWLEDGMENTS:

A loving thank you to my tolerant family and to friends, too numerous to list, who believed in me and repeatedly restored my self-confidence. I am especially grateful also for the many hours of research contributed by Roy Meier ("baby Roy" in this book) who still lives in that same house, and the lengthy letters from Len Meier. Without their help this book could not have been written with authenticity.

Maywood, Ill. JEANETTE GILGE

Contents

Another Verleger

Her left coat pocket was empty. Sure enough. Ellen had lost one mitten, just as Mama had predicted. She stood arms akimbo, skinny long legs planted ungracefully apart and watched the giggling, shoving, toe-treading girls don their wraps and tear out of the door as though they expected the shabby little school house to burst into flames at any moment.

When the door slammed behind the last muffler-wound figure she dropped to her knees and groped in the dim corners of the coat room. Mama's voice rang in her ears. "After you've lost those mittens you'll wish they had been on a string," Mama had said when Ellen insisted she did not want the mittens Mama had just knitted for her put on a crocheted string.

"I'm thirteen, Mama. I don't have to have them dangling out of my sleeves like a little kid," she had protested.

Surprisingly, Mama hadn't argued. She merely shrugged

and said, "All right. But you'll end up losing them. Wait and see."

In a little space behind the coat room door Ellen's fingers closed tightly over the rough homespun mitten. "Once. Just once couldn't I be right instead of Mama?" she mumbled as she yanked it on, grabbed her lunch pail and ran outside.

The wind whipped her breath away as she rounded the corner of the school house and trudged over the icy path to the road without looking up. She stepped out on the sleigh-tracked road expecting to see eight-year-old Minnie patiently waiting, but she saw only four heads bobbing out of sight over the crest of the hill. Ed's disappeared first, Minnie's next, then Len's and finally George's.

What luck to be able to walk home alone without Minnie jabbering all the way. Ellen checked an impulse to let out an elated yell by reminding herself that a thirteen-year-old girl simply does not whoop and holler like a boy. Anyway, she shouldn't feel so happy because Minnie went on ahead of her. Wasn't she only too happy to have Minnie as an ally against seven brothers when they teased her? Three-year-old Gertie wasn't much help.

Still, she didn't have to feel guilty about wanting to be alone so she could think—not after what she had heard Mama say one evening last week. She was up in her room when Papa's voice drifted up the stairway.

"Emma? What's the matter with that girl? She can't wait to run up to her room every chance she gets."

Mama hadn't answered immediately. Ellen held her breath and listened to Mama's rocker squeak a few times. Then Mama said, "Nothing's wrong with her, Al. I remember when I was her age. Seemed like I never had enough time to be alone to try to fit things together."

"Things?"

"You know—feelings and ideas and what life is all

10

about." There was another pause and Mama said, "She's got a right to have some time alone."

Papa had only grunted in reply but Ellen felt relieved when he said no more about it. She'd wanted to run right down and hug Mama for being so understanding. Why couldn't she feel warm and loving toward Mama all the time? She groaned and the wind snatched it and carried it away. "One minute I feel loving and the next I'd like to kick her in the shins," she muttered. "I don't deserve a good mother like Mama." For punishment she made herself walk in one narrow sleigh track. It wasn't easy to balance on that icy strip but she painstakingly placed one foot directly in front of the other all the way down the Benson hill, thinking how it reminded her of the narrow way Pastor Voss talked about in confirmation class. Her knees trembled at the very thought of Pastor Voss shouting that anyone who hates his brother is a murderer and that "brother" means sister, parents, teachers, neighbors—*everyone!* Ellen groaned again. She was a murderer as surely as if she had shouldered Papa's rifle and pulled the trigger—not only at Mama but at a good many other people as well. If Pastor Voss knew how she glared at Mama's back when Mama made her angry and how she felt like kicking her in the shins he might put her right out of the class! Why couldn't she be like Minnie? Minnie never glared at Mama's back no matter how much Mama scolded and hollered.

"But Mama doesn't scold anyone as much as she scolds me," Ellen protested out loud. It felt so good to talk right out loud about how she felt that she talked all the while she walked the level stretch between the bottom of the Benson hill and the top of what everyone called "the maple hill," confident that the howl of the wind obliterated her words so no one would hear how hard it was to be the oldest girl in a family of ten children and how exasperating it was to hear Mama scold all the time. "If she would only talk and laugh with me like she does with Mrs. Geber and Aunt Clara," she mumbled into her muffler. It was so nice to see Mama throw back her head and let the laughter roll out from some deep place where she stored it for special occasions. Ellen smiled just thinking about that laugh and she felt warm and loving toward Mama, like she did when one of the little ones said something funny and Mama'd catch Papa's eye and they'd exchange a smile. Ellen's heart gave a little flip when she saw Mama and Papa look at each other like that.

Her heart gave that same little flip when she watched Mama soothe a crying baby. Love seemed to pour right out of her—like when she sat peacefully rocking and knitting (how would Mama look without knitting in her hands?) and smiling at the lighted candles on the Christmas tree.

Christmas! Elation washed over her. Not even two weeks and there'd be skating on the river, coasting on the hills—maybe even at night—and she'd go to Emma Geber's house and Emma Ehrlich's and they'd talk and giggle and eat Christmas candy and just have fun. Ellen whirled around and around—not caring anymore where she stepped, and just to be different she took the left branch of the road that ran around the base of the three huge maple trees instead of the right one.

Where the road rejoined she stopped to watch the wind blow two columns of smoke over the treetops a quarter of a mile farther down the gently sloping hill—Olafson's smoke on the left of the road, Verleger's on the right. The right column gave an extra little puff. Maybe Mama had just given the heater stove grates a hearty shaking.

Halfway down the slope where Richter's woods ended the house came into view. The audacity of it to stand there so serenely—belying the teaming activity within its walls!

She smiled remembering the thrill that had swept through her when she reached this spot that first fall after the house was built and saw the evening sun turn the new shingles to gold. Three years of weathering had softened that gold to silvery gray, but Ellen's pride remained undimmed. Soon, she supposed, frame houses would replace all the log cabins in the German settlement—but for now the Verleger house was unique.

Papa must be so proud when he looks down from this spot on the road and sees the house and all the cleared land, she thought. She could see the dim outline of the little log cabin against the dark trees across the field to her right. Here on the river bank Papa had built a log barn and cabin and cleared land for the first field and a garden in 1886—seventeen years ago. Each succeeding year Papa had cut more trees, dug out more stubborn stumps, plowed more land and gauged success by the number of acres under plow. Even now in 1903 Ellen heard the men talk more about how many acres they had under plow than how many head of stock they owned.

Now sixteen-year-old Al and fourteen-year-old Fred worked beside Papa and each year more acres took the place of tangled woods than the year before.

"Looks like our hardest years are over, Emma," Papa said with a sigh of satisfaction at the supper table one night as he looked around the table encircled with fast-growing children. "No limit to what we can do with all this energy." He proceeded to outline plans for the coming months radiating enthusiasm like the glowing heater stove radiated heat. One was obliged to absorb it.

But Papa didn't believe in praise. He considered the satisfaction of seeing a job well done ample reward—except when he smiled a special smile of approval that was worth much more than words. To kindle that special smile was Ellen's daily goal. Only rarely had she ever attained it.

A spark of dormant enthusiasm flared and Ellen stumbled over the bumpy path across the front yard determined to work uncomplainingly. Maybe, if she tried extra hard, one day Mama might even smile a special approving smile.

At the kitchen door she took a deep breath of delicious cold air, exhaled a white cloud and watched the wind wisk it away. Hand on the door knob she hesitated, fearing her new determination would be blown away as completely as her breath as soon as Mama said, "Now go change your dress and put on an apron." Ellen *always* changed her dress and put on an apron but Mama *always* had to say it. She gritted her teeth. "I'm not going to let her make me angry," she muttered and opened the door.

But the big kitchen was empty—the whole house quiet except for the tick of the pendulum clock on the shelf to the left of the door. Four syrup pails stood on the big white oilcloth-covered table. Ellen set her lunch pail down beside them. No wonder Minnie had been in such a hurry to get home. The hill back of the barn must be just right for coasting. Ellen had heard Minnie and the boys squabbling over the big sled back there when she came across the yard.

Ellen peeked into the front room to Mama's bedroom door. Not a sound. She couldn't see Mama's bed from where she stood but she could see little bumps under the patchwork quilt in the homemade bed where John, Gertie and little Roy napped. If she hurried—and was ever so quiet—she might make it upstairs before Mama woke up. She could daydream about Christmas or maybe read a story in *The Youth's Companion*.

Way on the end hook, as far as possible from where Papa and the big boys would hang their coats that smelled like horses and barn, Ellen hung her coat. She shivered. Better not let the fire go out. Cautiously she lifted the heavy iron stove lid. Good bed of coals, thank goodness!

She reached for a stick of wood and started when a little roll of white outing flannel scraps bounced off the wood box edge. Mama must have been sewing and left it there. She shoved wood in the stove, snatched up the flannel roll and squeezed it tight. It couldn't be. It just *couldn't* be. Not yet! Little Roy wouldn't be a year old until the day after Christmas. She opened her fist and let the scraps fall into the fire, scowling at the unmistakable outlines of a baby sacque. Flames licked at the edges and crept over them, leaving velvet-black fragments that writhed in the heat. She watched with morbid fascination then stifled the urge to slam the lid, replaced it soundlessly and tiptoed upstairs and dove far under the heavy quilts. "Darn it!" she muttered into her flour-sack pillow case, "We don't need another baby. Ten kids are enough. We'll never get the work done when a new baby comes." She groaned at the thought of Mama dragging herself around grunting and panting and crabby as the dickens.

Out came her nose for a breath of air and back under she went for another tirade after she had made a dome of the quilts to protect her big red hair bow. Maybe she should take off her shoes. No. Mama might call anytime and she hated to button shoes, especially with cold fingers. Better leave them on so she'd be ready to run downstairs when Mama called. She gave her pillow a punch. "Now I'll never get over to Emma Geber's or even out coasting. But what really makes me angry is that Mama won't say one word about the baby coming—like she's ashamed of having a baby. Makes no sense at all. She's sure proud of her babies once they get here. Can just see how it will be. All of a sudden one day Papa'll send Al to get Mrs. Geber and he'll shoo us outside to play—or in the barn if it's bad weather—and a long while later he'll call us—all proud and smiling and tell us to come and see the new baby. I'll have to stay home from school and help with the work

15

'cause Mrs. Geber has her own work to do. Why'd I have to be the oldest girl anyhow?"

Ellen threw the covers back and sat up. Her face scowled back from the mirror. Just hate it when Mama is up again sitting there nursing the baby looking like an old owl with those black rings under her eyes. I wish we'd never get another baby!

"Ella? You up there?" Mama called.

"I'm coming!" Ellen yelled, sniffing the delicious aroma of onions being sliced over the venison roast.

Mama didn't look up when Ellen came down. She sat furiously peeling potatoes. Her hair straggled out of the tight pug she wore at the back of her head and creases from sleeping showed clearly on her right cheek.

"Ella! Get the rest of the washing in right away," she yelled over a chorus of cries and whimpers.

Minnie yanked at five-year-old John's boots while he bawled like a tortured calf. Three-year-old Gertie howled somewhere under the table and little Roy clung to Mama's long gathered skirt crying simply because everyone else was crying.

"Ella, why on earth didn't you wake me? Look at John! He's half frozen." She shook her head. "He woke up and went out coasting and I never even heard him get up. If he ain't sick after coughing all last night . . ." She tucked a stray lock of hair into her pug and motioned to John with her paring knife. "You go sit close to the heater stove and get good and warm. Minnie! Take the baby so I can move. Ella! Put wood in the heater stove before you go out."

"The heater won't draw, Mama. The ashes are piled way up."

"Oh, for pity sakes! That's another thing I should have done. John, sit here by the cook stove but stay out of my way. Leave the ashes, Ella. Just get the clothes in before it's pitch dark out there."

16

Out at the clothes line Ellen wrenched clothes pins off the frozen clothes, knowing that the underwear and over-alls would hang woodenly on the line even without clothes pins. With numb fingers she lifted the clothes off the line and laid them over the clothes basket in a grotesque heap. Only the second week in December. Even if the baby didn't come for awhile there would still be weeks and weeks of cold weather and dozens of frozen diapers. Ellen grabbed the cumbersome pile and scrunched her way over the bumpy path and fumbled for the door knob.

Mama flung the door open, breathing fast from hurry-ing. "Just set them down by the stove till they soften a little and I'll hang them behind the stove later. Goodness, girl, you're cold. Warm your hands slow now or they'll really hurt."

Ellen glared at Mama's back. If she wasn't so darn considerate, Ellen thought as she pulled off her coat, I could be angry without feeling guilty. She bit her lip, accepting the pain of her warming hands as penance for her ugly thoughts.

A rush of cold air! Three snow-covered boys scuffled on the floor.

"Stop that commotion!" Mama yelled. "George, carry out the heater stove ashes. Ed! Len! Fill the wood boxes. Quick now!"

Ed, the smallest, scrambled on the floor trying to grab Len's feet, but big George held his wet mittens over Ed's eyes while Ed panted and struggled.

"I said quit that!"

The scuffling continued.

Mama caught the back of George's coat collar and yanked hard. "Do I always have to get mad before you boys mind me?" Veins stood out on her neck and her face was red.

Mama was hardly back at the stove when they went at it

again. In one deft move she grabbed a stick of kindling wood and took after them. They bolted out the door and slammed it so hard the windows rattled. With a sigh she tossed the stick back in the box, wiped her hands on her apron and began to grind coffee. "Open a two-quart jar of *Gherkins,* Ella," she called over the roar of the grinder. "Minnie, set the table."

The boys staggered in, arms loaded with wood, and left the door open. Freezing air swirled around Ellen's ankles and sent shivers racing over her body, but before she could close it Papa, Al and Fred stomped in—their faces glowing from the long day in the cold woods.

"It'll hit twenty below tonight," Papa predicted, pulling off his leather mitts.

Mama hung her head. "Supper ain't ready yet."

Papa looked questioningly at Mama and pulled his mitts back on.

Mama looked up at him with a shy little smile and whispered, "Overslept!"

Her eyes held his until he gave her a reassuring wink and she bustled back to work.

"Might as well feed first," he said with a shrug. "Al! Fred! Supper ain't ready. We'll feed first." He strode out leaving them struggling back into their coats and grumbling.

Al reached over to swipe a slice of bread Ellen was slicing. She rapped his knuckles with the dull edge of the knife without looking up.

"Ma! Ma! She tried to cut my fingers off!" he howled in mock anguish. Ellen knew he was grinning.

Ignoring him, Mama quickly spread a slice of bread with soft butter, tore it in half and slipped the pieces to Al and Fred. "Get going now," she whispered, "before they all want some."

When the door slammed behind them she frowned at

Ellen. "Shame on you! Don't hurt none to give those big hungry boys something to eat when they come in half starved. How'd you like to be out in that freezing woods all day?" Mama went to the front room to call Minnie, and Ellen glared at her back again wishing she'd be mean and selfish—just once.

By the time Papa and the boys came back from the barn Mama and Ellen were ready to dish up the steaming potatoes, venison, gravy and carrots. Ed, Len and George slid into their places on the bench behind the table and elbowed each other while Minnie, Gertie and John settled themselves on the front bench. Papa swung his right leg over his chair seat, grasped the front edge of the seat and pulled the chair up under him. Nobody but Papa ever sat down like that, Ellen thought. No one but a very tall man could sit down like that.

Mama sat down with a groan and pulled little Roy up on her lap. She always fed the baby from her plate. Al and Fred scooted in on the back bench, and Ellen sat at the end opposite Papa so she could refill bowls and pour coffee.

When Al handed her the empty potato bowl she had taken only one bite of potatoes and gravy. She managed to cut her meat and get several more bites before she had to cut more bread. When she sat down again the venison was cold and tallow coated her mouth. She scowled at the boys eating their second helpings of nice hot food without interruption. But, as the talk of hemlock bark and logs and tanneries and skidding and thaws went on and on she was content to be a girl.

After supper Mama had to get after George and Len and Ed before they got the reservoir filled, the slop pail carried out and a fresh pail of water carried in. It was Ed, his pixie ears rosy with cold, who lugged in the pail of water,

19

took a noisy drink and dropped the dipper back in the pail instead of hanging it up.

Little Roy was right behind him. Gleefully, he seized the rare opportunity to grab the handle of the dipper. His shriek as the icy water sloshed over his front brought Mama out of the pantry so fast she had to hold the door frame to keep her balance.

"There! There! Mama'll get you nice and dry. Who left that dipper in the pail anyhow?" she yelled, but there was no one in sight but Ellen scowling at the tallow-coated roasting pan. "Here, I'll scrub that. You put Roy's nightie on him. As soon as I'm done I'll rock him. Just must take time to rock him—he's still just a baby."

Although taking care of little Roy seemed preferable to washing the roasting pan, Ellen was in no mood to be mollified. The sooner she could get up to her room the better she'd like it. As soon as they were out of Mama's sight she gave him a good jerk. "Brat!" she said and yanked his nightie over his head.

"Peek!" he chirped with an undaunted grin as his head popped out.

She hugged him close. "Oh, you . . ." she whispered against his moist little neck. God sure knows what He's doing when He makes babies so adorable, she thought.

Snug in bed a little while later, Ellen rolled over on her stomach and pulled the quilts hoodlike over her head. Stars blinked through the upper sections of the window-panes where the frost had melted during the day and opaque frost-flowers grew again in the evening chill.

Earlier in the day Ellen had planned to daydream about anticipated pleasures—coasting on moonlit nights, visiting with the Emmas, practicing for the Christmas program at school and the magic of the program night, and Mama sitting in the audience looking blissfully happy listening to the Christmas carols like she was glimpsing a bit of heaven and listening to an angel chorus—and of pleasant conversations with Miss McKinley. Oh how she loved to talk with her after school and at recess and hear about cities and places far away from the German settlement.

But now her thoughts rolled around like a marble in a bowl. A bowl with a hollow in the bottom where the unpleasant thoughts about the new baby persistently lodged. She tried to think of pleasant things but back her thoughts would go—into the hollow.

No use! Might as well face it. That baby'll be here as certainly as Christmas—or would it? She shook off the quilts and sat up. She could lose it! Not long ago she had overheard Mrs. Geber and Mama talking about someone losing a baby and Mrs. Geber had said nearly everyone loses at least one—sometimes several.

Ellen ducked her head under the quilts to hide a sly smile. Maybe Mama would lose this one. There was a chance. . . . Minnie pounced on her and her smile vanished. Time to go to sleep.

The next thing she knew Papa was shaking down the cook stove ashes. It was morning.

Shivering so violently she could hardly button up, Ellen wished she was still little like Minnie and Gertie who dressed down by the cook stove with their backsides cozy warm while they sat on the big iron oven door and pulled their stockings up over long underwear legs and buttoned their shoes—while *Minnie* buttoned their shoes. Gertie was too young to manage Mama's ivory-handled button hook.

Mama gave her usual morning weather report while Ellen splashed her face with icy water in an effort to wake herself up. "Looks like it's going to be a nice day. Windy though. Sure hope we don't get a good blizzard before Christmas."

Still drowsy, her hands barely able to do her bidding, Ellen helped Mama spread slice after slice of bread with jelly or syrup for the school children and for the men to take to the woods. (Al, 16, and Fred, 14, were considered men when it came to work; boys when it came to making decisions.)

"I'm sure going to have to get a move on this week," Mama said. "Let's see . . . today's Tuesday. Friday is the Christmas program already and you kids are out of school. Can sure use you and Minnie around here." She shook her head. "But those boys!" She loaded unwrapped sandwiches into syrup pails. "Don't forget to press the hair ribbons. Are you listening to me, Ella?"

"Yes, Mama," Ellen answered and retreated back into her own thoughts. Mama just *had* to talk in the morning. It'd be worse if she was crabby, Ellen reminded herself, but why does she have to always talk about the weather? Can't change it anyhow. And how can she be so cheerful knowing pretty soon she'll be up night after night with a new baby?

"Ella! Wake up now. You've been spreading that slice for five minutes."

"Have not!" she snapped.

"That will do, young lady," Mama said in a tone of voice one didn't challenge. But when Mama turned to put wood in the stove Ellen glared at her. "Hate being called 'Ella,' " she said to herself. "Why'd they give me a pretty name like 'Ellen' and then go and call me 'Ella'?" She had asked Mama several times if they couldn't please call her "Ellen" and Mama said she didn't know why not. But in a day or two they'd all be calling her "Ella" again. "Ellen" reminded her of a picture she had once seen of a slim-waisted girl sitting under a blossoming apple tree wearing a lovely wide-brimmed hat, while "Ella" made her think of a stocky girl in blue denim scrubbing a pine floor with lye soap. Of course she liked it when Papa called her "Ellie." The boys sometimes called her "Ellie" too, but when they

22

did she knew they wanted her to talk Mama into letting them make taffy or popcorn.

All the way to school that morning—with Minnie panting along beside her—she thought of herself as "Ellen." At least she had a slim waist and nice skin. Last summer she had heard Mrs. Stuhl tell Mama that Ellen had pretty skin and wanted to know if she used something special on it. Mama had sounded pleased but assured her that all Ellen ever used was plain soap and water. For a time Ellen had felt so good knowing she had pretty skin that she almost forgot about her protruding teeth. Mama said they were *not* buck teeth, even if the boys said they were. But she was terribly conscious of them and had a habit of propping up her arm and pushing against her teeth with her fist when she studied in school. Almost daily she leaned close to the mirror over her dresser and examined them, trying to convince herself that the pressure was forcing them back. Then, a few weeks ago, she confided to Miss McKinley that she thought her teeth were ugly. Miss McKinley said she had a slight overbite but that she had never even noticed it until Ellen had called her attention to it. At first Ellen was joyously reassured but after a few days she decided to keep pushing just to make sure. Maybe Miss McKinley was simply being kind.

What really bothered her was that she was the only one in the family who had teeth like that—and no one else had wiry hair like hers either. Oh, it was about the same shade of brown as Mama's, but Mama's was soft and fine. Ellen's sprang stubbornly out of her braids and attempted to curl no matter how tightly she braided it. Another thing that bothered her was that she didn't have the deep dimple in her chin like Papa's, either. Everyone else did, except baby Roy, but maybe his would look deeper when he got older. Maybe she wasn't even . . ."Ella?" Minnie yelled over the whistling wind. "Think Miss McKinley'll make us do lessons all day? Think she'll let us practice for the program?"

"She might. Not all day though. Not till Thursday at least." Excitement surged through Ellen at the thought of the program and she gave Minnie a quick hug and chatted amiably the rest of the way to school.

Keeping more than thirty youngsters studying that day was like keeping thirty corks under water. Still Miss McKinley allowed practice only during singing class and noon hour. By noon Wednesday she relented and put everyone who wasn't busy performing to work making paper chains with precious bits of colored paper she had hoarded all year.

That night as Ellen was leaving Miss McKinley whispered, "I certainly hope the audience enjoys the program as much as the participants."

Ellen smiled and nodded—too flustered by Miss McKinley's confidential tone of voice to think of an answer. When Miss McKinley talked to her like that she felt positively grown up.

Her eyes squeezed shut as she struggled into her coat, Ellen could still see the yellow flecks in Miss McKinley's eyes. She could never quite decide what color they were. They changed with her moods—dark and piercing when she was angry—almost green when they sparkled with delight. And her hair—all piled high and smooth. Ellen shot a parting glance at Miss McKinley's shining head bent over her desk. Her hair looked dark brown now in the late evening light, but the brighter the light the more red it became till it glowed like a red halo when she was in bright sunshine. That's the way I'll fix my hair when I grow up, Ellen thought. I won't pull it back tight and flat like Mama's. I'll wear it piled high and smooth. I'll wear white high-necked ruffled blouses tucked into dark skirts, and I'll keep my waist nice and slim if I have to *starve*. Wonder what makes her smell so nice. Someday I'll think of a way to ask her what it is.

All the way home she thought about how she'd still be friends with Miss McKinley when she grew up and they'd sit and talk and sip tea out of dainty flowered cups. They'd talk about books and music and about all the places they'd like to see—not about babies and quilt patches and people's sicknesses like Mama and Mrs. Geber did.

Thursday they sang until their throats ached and at noon the big boys helped Miss McKinley suspend the makeshift stage curtains on a wire stretched across the front end of the room. Ellen frowned at the seamed flour-sack curtains dyed an uneven gray and wished for pretty bright blue ones hung by rings instead of ugly old safety pins. If she only had money she'd order them from Sears Roebuck.

Friday crawled by as children faltered over their recitations and Ellen was about to burst with impatience when Miss McKinley dismissed them an hour early so the older children could help her put up the Christmas tree.

When the last little one had been shooed out the door, the big boys brought in the tree and secured it in the homemade stand. They clipped the candle holders to the highest branches and then sat down to heckle the girls while they trimmed the tree.

"Oh, boys! I've never seen a more perfect tree," Miss McKinley exclaimed. The boys' ears turned red and they grinned. "Won't the children be excited when they see it tonight?" she said over her shoulder as she hurried to the storage room.

All eyes were on her when she came back with a brown box, set it down and carefully lifted the cover. A chorus of "oh's" surrounded her when the girls saw the shining colored glass balls. Candle drippings here and there from previous Christmases made them more precious to Ellen and she imagined how lovely the McKinleys' tree must look.

Hardly daring to breathe, fingers trembling a bit, they hung the lovely fragile ornaments in the most prominent spots.

"Will my mother ever love these!" Ellen called over the chatter.

"Oh! So will mine!" echoed the other girls.

A few more hours. Just a few more!

When the last candle had been straightened and the last paper chain draped on the tree, they admired the result—assuring each other this was the most beautiful tree to ever stand in this schoolroom.

Over the hard snow Ellen sped, the squeak, squeak, squeak of her footsteps breaking the evening silence. In just a few hours the big logging sleigh would carry them up this very hill, and the whole family'd pile out of the sleigh laughing and calling to neighbors as the fragrance of balsam rushed out to meet them every time someone opened the door. Yellow light from kerosene lamps hanging in wall brackets—reflectors freshly polished—would throw mysterious shadows on familiar walls and mercifully hide the scars of the shabby little room.

Ellen's pulse quickened at the thought of everyone rushing around in their best clothes—the boys smelling of hair tonic and the girls of talcum powder. And all those people! Enough to make you gasp the first time the curtains opened and you saw them all. But when Mama gave an almost imperceptible nod of approval accompanied by a reassuring smile, the flutters in Ellen's middle always subsided. Then one recitation or song would follow on the heels of another and before she was quite aware that this was *the* big night, the tree candles would make dancing shadows on the ceiling, the lamps would be blown out, and they'd sing "Silent Night" as ladies dabbed their eyes, gruff men blinked hard and little brothers and sisters sat wide-eyed and motionless. And Mama! She'd sit there with her head tilted a bit to her left, eyes glowing, smiling that blissful Christmas smile.

Ellen broke into a run as though it would help make the night come faster by getting home as soon as she could.

"Should be able to finish knitting this sock while you're gone tonight," Mama said, laying her knitting on the table after supper.

"You're not going to the program?"

"No . . . I don't want to take little Roy out. I—I think he's getting a cold."

"But, Mama!"

"Papa'll be there and so will Gertie and John. You can tell me all about it when you get home." Mama hurried into the pantry and Ellen fled upstairs to hide tears of disappointment and anger.

If Mama wasn't having that baby. . . . She took her new navy blue serge dress Mama had just finished sewing the night before out of the closet and laid it quickly on the bed, but not before a tear splashed down the front of it. She brushed it off and wiped her eyes on the sleeve of her school dress. No time to cry now. Minnie rushed in and she helped her dress, answering her chatter in monosyllables while a cold lump of fear gathered deep inside her. Something was wrong. Even last year when little Roy was about to be born Mama had gone to the program. She pulled her new dress over her head and knotted the red tie with trembling fingers. Mama must be sick.

Even the crystal clear starlit night left her unaffected as the sleigh moved slowly up the hill. She huddled deeper into the blankets and snuggled Gertie close to her and

27

swallowed repeatedly to ease the lump in her throat.

At school she was caught up in the excitement in spite of herself but when she looked out at the audience where Mama should be sitting, faces blurred through tears. She concentrated on Papa's less expressive but comforting face throughout the program and found herself enjoying both performing and listening to the others, but when "Silent Night" had been sung she rushed into the dim coat room and had a quick cry while the younger children were receiving their sacks of candy from Miss McKinley. There'd be time to get hers later.

Mama looked rested and alert when they trouped in after the program. She laid her nearly completed sock down and gave them her full attention. Ellen sighed with relief. Maybe little Roy really *was* getting a cold.

"My goodness!" Mama exclaimed, clapping her hands, "you children must have been good to deserve so much candy and nuts!" She carefully chose a piece of hard candy from the many rattling bags they offered her. "Don't eat too much before bedtime," she warned. "You'll get a stomachache."

Everyone talked at once. Mama sucked the piece of candy and nodded and her eyes twinkled. When she smiled up at Papa a wave of happiness washed over Ellen, but her happiness was short-lived. They hadn't been home a half hour when Mama's eyes lost their sparkle and her smile became strained.

Papa saw it too. "Time for bed!" he ordered. "Enough excitement for one day." He motioned for Ellen to take Gertie to bed.

Long after everyone was asleep Ellen stared into the darkness. Mama didn't look like she was about to have a baby any day—maybe she could still lose it. Immediately guilt stabbed her. How awful to wish someone would lose a baby. Still . . . it hadn't sounded like something bad when Mrs. Geber had talked about it. Just so Mama wouldn't be sick or it wouldn't hurt or anything. . . . If Mama lost the baby she would be strong and bright-eyed and sing as she worked again, Ellen thought, wiggling deeper into her warm nest. No. It wasn't wrong to wish that Mama would feel well and strong. The clock struck two. Ellen sighed and slept.

Before dawn Sunday morning a blizzard descended. At daylight the barn was barely visible through the whirling snow.

"I won't even try to meet Reverend Voss today," Papa told Mama as he pulled his collar high up around his ears before he went out to do chores.

Once a month the minister who lived twenty miles away in Tomahawk managed to get a ride as far as Spirit Falls where he was met by one of the German settlement parishioners. Today it was Papa's turn to meet him and bring him the last eight miles to the new little frame church across the road from the schoolhouse. But Papa knew Pastor Voss would not start out today in this blizzard.

The little congregation of German Lutherans was almost three years old now, and Papa predicted that in the near future a minister would come every Sunday. "The only trouble with having church services every Sunday," Papa had said, "is that people will begin to take church for granted. The younger children will think we've always been able to go to church every Sunday."

Perhaps the younger children would think there had always been church services every Sunday, but Ellen would remember those exciting Sundays when Pastor Doripat had occasionally come from Butternut about forty miles away. He had even walked the last thirteen miles from Ogema when spring mud prevented horse and buggy travel. Ellen couldn't count the hours the congregation had waited for him. Sometimes he hadn't come at all but people didn't get upset. Opportunities to visit with neighbors were always welcome.

Like today. Ellen had looked forward to seeing Emma Geber and Emma Ehrlich, but now the work-filled week before Christmas loomed ahead without a single prospect of fun. The pelt of the snow against the windows and the howl of the wind made her angry instead of making her feel cozy and protected the way it usually did.

But time moves swiftly when one is busy, and as Ellen hung up the big gray dishpan Thursday night she realized that tomorrow night was Christmas Eve.

There had been so much to do she hadn't had time to be angry about the new baby or even concerned about Mama, although she felt her jaws tense each time Mama sat down with a groan leaving a task unfinished. Mama never stopped bossing though, and eventually the work got done.

The other day Mama had been *so* cross when Ellen had tried to enjoy cutting around the cardboard cookie patterns. Thank goodness Fred had patiently transferred the angels, gingerbread men, stars and Christmas tree shapes to the big black baking pans without marring them. Someday, Mama said, she'd buy regular cutters in fancy shapes but now she owned only a round one. It was back-breaking work cutting cookies but the children would enjoy them so much when they hung sparkling with sugar on the Christmas tree. Did Mama have to spoil it by telling them to hurry all the time? And for once Ellen had been sympathetic toward Minnie when Mama kept telling her to hurry while she was putting the countless hazelnut-sized *Pfeffernuesse* in baking pans, after Ellen had rolled long ropes of dough and cut the tiny pieces.

Ellen hung up the dish towel and stood idly warming her hands over the cook stove, remembering how the *Pfeffernuesse* had filled the house with a luscious spicy fragrance and how they had disappeared like corn in a hen coop as the boys sauntered through the kitchen on one pretext or other. At least Minnie had redeemed herself for all the times she had done nothing but get in the way this week. She had looked so sweet placing the *Pfeffernuesse* in the pans—her head moving back and forth, back and forth. She wore her hair parted in the middle and pulled severely back, exposing a large brown mole on her forehead. She could have hid it with a lock of hair but she chose to let it show. "God put it there," she told curious schoolmates, "why should I hide it?" Minnie's reasoning made no sense to Ellen, but then many things about Minnie made no sense to Ellen. One minute she could be singing and the next minute clattering upstairs in tears for no apparent reason. Though she lavished affection on the little ones, she stood rigid and unresponsive when Ellen or Mama hugged her. But when Ellen had praised her neat work with the *Pfeffernuesse* Minnie flashed her a radiant smile. Ellen vowed to praise Minnie more often. Why, *words* can make people happy! The thought thrilled her. Last week when they had read about people giving gifts wrapped in colored paper she had felt so dejected. It would be so much fun to give someone a real wrapped gift and watch them open it. Sometime when she grew up and earned money. . . . But now—she hugged herself delightedly—she'd use words to give happiness.

And it was Friday—Christmas Eve and she didn't feel like Christmas at all. Work. No end of it. It wouldn't be so bad if Mama was strong and singing her way through the day as she usually did, but to see her suddenly sit down, stifle a groan and look like she might cry any moment made Ellen angry one minute and concerned the next. Just before supper she found Mama in the pantry wiping tears on her apron. "Must be getting a cold," she had said with an exaggerated sniff, then waddled out of the pantry. But

Ellen knew Mama had been crying.

All during supper Ellen wanted to cry, and she realized while she was washing dishes that she hadn't made anyone smile all day by saying something nice. It had seemed like such a wonderful idea. Why hadn't she been able to carry it out? Tears were imminent when Papa brought in a bundle of cedar boughs and dropped them on the table.

"Found some with the little cones you like, Emma."

Mama gave him a tiny smile and snapped off a sprig and laid it on the cook stove. In a moment the fresh cedar fragrance drifted through the house. "Ah! Now it smells like Christmas," Mama said, closing her eyes and inhaling deeply.

Like magic the cedar fragrance evoked scenes and emotions of other Christmases. Bits and fragments of past pleasures—dreamlike in their confusion, but they dissipated her concern and sadness and filled her heart with the ultimate joy of Christmas, that the Savior was born—filled her to overflowing and she wanted to shout, to laugh, to cry—all at the same time. She scooped bewildered little Gertie into her arms and whirled around the room. "It's Christmas Eve, *Liebchen*. The night the *Christkindchen* was born!" Gertie ran in circles squealing with excitement when Ellen put her down, and Ellen danced back to the dishpan and began singing "Joy to the World" at the top of her voice. Little John came out of the front room where he had been playing with empty spools and looked at Ellen like she had taken leave of her senses. Mama nodded and smiled and joined in singing—catching an extra breath here and there. One by one the other children appeared and joined in, and Papa and the big boys added their bass to the last verse.

It wasn't easy to subdue the excited children but eventually when even the school-age boys were in bed

Papa brought in the crackling cold tree. "Had an eye on this one all year. Wait till we get it set up!"

Al and Fred helped him whittle the trunk to fit the hole in the stand he had made of crossed two-by-fours.

While they set up the tree, Mama and Ellen stuck cedar boughs behind every picture on the walls—even behind the wavy wood-framed mirror above the kitchen wash-stand.

"It *is* a beauty!" Mama exclaimed, bending boughs down that were still inclined to point upward after lying in the cold. "Mmm! I love the smell of freshly cut balsam," she said, and went to get the box of ornaments from her bedroom.

Papa sat down and stretched his long legs out so close to the heater stove that his homespun socks steamed. "Come sit down, Emma. Let's just boss this year."

Ever so carefully Ellen unpacked the ornaments and silently greeted each one like an old friend. When Fred and Al began hanging them carelessly she wailed, "Hang them where they *show*!"

"Oh, hang your old ornaments yourself," Al growled. "Fred and I'll hang the cookies and the popcorn strings."

She took her time hanging the few bright balls and the tinsel twisted with wire in the shapes of crescents and stars, then stood back and studied them critically and changed some to more prominent positions.

Meanwhile the boys had attached the candle holders and Ellen sniffed the box of new candles Papa had brought from Tomahawk. "Don't you *love* the smell of new candles?" she asked Mama, holding the candles under Mama's nose.

"Sure do. I like the smell after they've been blown out, too." She smiled at Ellen and turned to Papa. "That's about the prettiest tree we've had for years. Wish we could save it for next year."

Papa beamed.

Al clipped on the last candle holder. "Pa? Can we light the candles—just for a couple minutes?"

Papa nodded and dug a match out of his pocket for Al, then one for himself and scratched it under the rocker seat and brought it up to his face only to discover he hadn't put his pipe in his mouth. The look on his face. . . .

Ellen couldn't remember when she had seen Mama laugh so hard. Mama wiped her eyes on her apron, caught her breath and burst out laughing again. "If you knew how funny you looked!" she gasped.

Papa laughed and put his pipe in his mouth with a flourish, struck another match, took a long draw and said, "Go ahead. Light the candles."

When all the candles were lit Ellen blew out the lamp and stood squinting and tilting her head first to the right, then to the left so that the myriad rays of light swung in intriguing arcs.

"Ella! What on earth are you doing?" Mama asked.

Ellen explained and they all tried it—squinting and tilting their heads.

Fred stopped first. "My gosh! We look like a bunch of idiots!"

Papa chuckled. "If somebody walked in they'd say, 'Always knew that Verleger family was a little off.' Well, boys, you better blow 'em out now so I don't have to put new ones in before morning."

Ellen watched the tendrils of smoke fade away, feeling so full of love she simply had to let some come out. She bent over Mama sitting with her head against the high-backed rocker and kissed her cheek. "Merry Christmas, Mama!"

Mama patted her shoulder. "Merry Christmas, my girl."

Ellen leaned over the back of Papa's rocker and rested her cheek briefly on the top of his head—she couldn't imagine *kissing* Papa. "Merry Christmas, Papa!"

Papa looked up at her and even in the pale light from the kitchen lamp Ellen could see the depth of feeling in his eyes. Tears brimming she ran upstairs. "Oh, Papa, if you could only say what you feel," she whispered. But then, seeing Papa's eyes again in the darkness she didn't mind not hearing words. As long as Papa looked at her like that—even if it was only at Christmas time, she'd be happy. With a sigh and a smile she snuggled deep under the quilts thinking of the lovely tree downstairs—its tinsel shimmering in the glow of the heater stove fire that shone through the isinglass door. She listened to Mama and Papa putting out the Christmas gifts and talking in companionable tones punctuated with occasional muffled laughs. Wonderful secure feelings enveloped her like a down-soft coverlet in the dark and quiet.

It seemed only moments later Papa was shaking down the ashes and putting wood in the stoves. The realization that it was Christmas Day spread through her like milk through a sugar lump. Down there under the tree she knew bowls of ribbon candy, peanuts, mixed nuts, and chocolate drops stood waiting for eager fingers. Surely Mama had piled carefully polished, hard, juicy store apples in the cut glass bowl she called "the bowl with the foot." Mama always put apples in that bowl. There were presents down there, too—clothes for the big children and a pair of homespun socks or mittens Mama had knitted for each one of them, and a toy for each of the younger children.

"It's Christmas!" one of the boys yelled and many feet hit the floor. Minnie tumbled out of bed and ran out into the hallway, but Ellen dressed as fast as she could before she joined them where they huddled against the warm chimney waiting for Fred and Al. Ed, Len and George shoved and bickered and stepped on Minnie's toes and made her cry. She stopped abruptly when Fred came out of his room hoisting his suspenders over his shoulders followed by tousle-headed Al. Al smothered a yawn and said, "All set? Let's go!" and they thundered down the stairs.

Mama, her hair still in a braid, sat in the rocker holding sleepy little Roy. Papa stood in his stocking feet rubbing his hands over the heater stove, and grinned at the excited youngsters. Gertie and John, still in their nighties, sat huddled together on the oven door.

At the door to the front room the group halted as though the lighted tree would vanish if they went any closer. Ellen's eyes flew from face to face. Many times she'd see the tree lighted these next few days but never again could she see these little faces reflect the same awe and joy that they felt this moment. If only such a moment could be preserved—suspended in time. . . . The school boys broke away first. Shouts turned to mumbles as they crammed their mouths with candy. Someone placed Gertie's rag doll in her arms and she hugged it close—her eyes still on the Christmas tree. Minnie squatted, skirt stretched tightly over her knees—a bulge of candy in her cheek— trying to decide what to sample next. Al and Fred watched the younger ones—just as Ellen did—probably wishing, like Ellen, that they were little again, all dazzled and amazed.

Ellen bent to pick up her new hair ribbons and dress goods. "Fred! Al! Look!" she whispered. She cradled two bright red candy cherries in her hand—one on each end of a wire hung over a branch.

"Hey!" Fred yelled. "There's lots of 'em."

Ellen stood up. Sure enough. There were candy cherries here and there all over the tree, but that wasn't all. She pointed questioningly to an angel-shaped cookie with pink frosting and sprinkled with tiny colored beads.

"They must have ordered them from Steinmeyer's in

Milwaukee," Al whispered. "Look. There's a lamb and a deer . . . they wanted to have a surprise for us, too."

And there were Mama and Papa smiling and watching them the way they had watched the little ones.

"Hey. What's that red thing way back there?" Papa said, pointing under the tree.

Eddie scrambled under the tree and dragged out a package wrapped in bright red tissue paper and tied with a narrow white ribbon. "It says 'To Emma from Al'," Eddie said, looking puzzled.

"It's to Mama from Papa, dummy!" George said, giving him a push toward Mama.

Eddie stumbled toward Mama and put it on her knees.

Maybe it was the reflection of the red paper that made Mama's face look so pink but Ellen doubted it. "Well, for goodness' sake! It's so pretty I just hate to open it," she said, fingering the bow.

"Open it! Open it!" everyone yelled, and the little ones jumped and giggled with excitement.

It was quiet then—except for the rustle of the paper and the snap of the fire as everyone watched Mama remove the paper and carefully fold it. "It's awfully heavy," she said, lifting the brown box that was about the size of one of her big loaves of bread. Ellen's heart beat faster. A real wrapped package. It didn't matter that it was Mama's and not hers. Not one bit. She could still share the suspense of wondering what was in it. Mama shook it. Tantalizing them.

"Open it, Mama!" they yelled.

She lifted the lid. Crumpled newspaper. She took out several pieces and then there was something wrapped in newspaper—an unfamiliar wood and metal object. She smiled and quickly groped in the box and lifted out a larger object and tore off the paper. "An iron—with a detachable handle." Her voice went up high. "Just like the one I saw in Olehoffen's store in Tomahawk last summer."

Papa chuckled, "That's just where it came from. When I told Mamie Dewing it was your Christmas present she wrapped it all up nice like that."

"Well I never . . ." Mama shook her head. "You be sure to thank her for me next time you go to town." Mama ran her hand over the sleek black finish of the iron and clipped the handle off and on. "See, it's pointed at both ends so you can get into gathers either way."

"Sure you got everything out of that box?" Papa asked.

Mama dug again. One . . . two more irons. "See," she explained, "two can be heating on the stove while you're ironing with the third one. What will they think of next?"

Minnie hopped up and down beside Mama. "Ain't you happy, Mama?"

Mama patted her arm. "I sure am! I never expected to get an iron with a detachable handle—not for a long time."

The room hummed again as everyone went back to his own gifts. Ellen wondered if Mama wished she had more to give Papa than the socks and wristlets she had knitted for him. She always knit wristlets with a loop for over the thumb to wear under his mittens because Papa's arms were too long for any coat he could buy and his wrists got cold.

Daylight slipped in unnoticed. The candles burned low and were blown out. Everyone but the three little ones turned reluctantly to their waiting chores.

"Mama, don't you wish we could hang onto Christmas morning for a whole day?" Ellen said with a sigh as she stirred the oatmeal.

Mama nodded and kept on slicing bread. "I think heaven will be like that. Here we get little snatches of happiness that slip right out of our grasp, but in heaven they will just go on and on." Mama sliced three more slices of bread and turned to Ellen—knife suspended in midair. "I'll tell you one way a person can hold onto happy times." She leaned closer to Ellen. "You think back over them—real hard—see it all again in your mind's eye—hear it all again and you'll remember it." She sliced another slice of bread. "Tell you something else," she said, shaking the knife at Ellen. "Anything you *don't* want to remember, like something horrid you saw, or something mean someone said—don't let yourself think about it again. If you start thinking about it, stop! It ain't easy and you got to erase it off your mind's eye like chalk off a blackboard. If you do that you won't have your mind all cluttered up with bad things that crowd out the good ones. You'll be mighty glad you got those good things to think about when you have to be alone a lot with nothing but your own thoughts for company."

"Do you *always* keep from thinking about bad things?"

"Oh, dear me, no! But I just keep trying 'cause I figure even a few bad things kept out of my mind is a big help."

That night before she went to sleep Ellen tried extra hard to remember every good thing about Christmas day—to see it all again, to hear it and even smell it. It was easy to remember the little ones with the candles reflected in their eyes when they saw the tree—and Mama opening her present. She saw the candy, the shiny apples—and George quartering one with his new knife and sharing it with John instead of chomping down a whole one. And Len—she could have hugged him.

"Hey, Ellie," he had said. "Wanna try my new mouth organ?"

She blew a few notes and was about to hand it back to him when she saw the dent where she had stepped on it after Christmas *last* year. Len shrugged and grinned. "What the heck," he said and marched away lustily blowing George's last year's Christmas gift.

Scene after scene paraded before Ellen's eyes. Then

39

came a jolt as she recalled an overheard conversation between Mrs. Geber and Mama. The Gebers had come to visit that afternoon, and when Ellen went to get Emma's coat from Mama's bed when they were leaving she heard Mrs. Geber say to Mama, "I tell you, Emma. I don't like it at all. Something just ain't right." Ellen couldn't hear Mama's answer, but when they came out Mama's eyes were red.

What had Mrs. Geber meant? It seemed like they were referring to Mama—but it could have been about something else. Anyway, Ellen preferred not to think about it tonight. She turned over and watched ribbon candy, chocolate drops and pink-frosted cookies float by until she fell asleep.

Time to Daydream

Even before breakfast was over the day after Christmas Ellen knew it would be a helter-skelter day. Papa and the boys would do only essential chores, and she and Mama would have to step over their long legs all day.

"I'm cooking a big pot of soup for supper," Mama said, pouring water on some beef bones. "They'll eat nuts and candy all day and we'll have little Roy's birthday cake tonight. That should fill them up."

At supper time all eyes were on little Roy when Ellen brought his whipped cream-covered cake to the table. He squealed at the lighted Christmas tree candle in the middle, and when Mama fed him some he reached out and got a fist full of whipped cream and everyone laughed. Ellen ran to get a wash cloth to wipe his sticky hands and face so Mama wouldn't have to get up. When she washed his face he squirmed away but gave her a forgiving grin, and she kissed his moist little cheek and whispered to Mama,

"Doesn't he have the prettiest blue eyes you ever saw?"

Mama nodded and leaned toward Ellen. "You know who has pretty blue eyes?" she said low enough so no one else paid any attention. "Henry Geber. Fred and Max are good-looking boys, but Henry is the handsome one."

"That smart aleck!" Ellen quipped. She hurried away hoping her face wasn't flushed. Henry's eyes weren't just pretty. They were magnets that held hers until she blushed and forced herself to look away. All the while she washed dishes she thought about Henry until Fred stuck his head in the doorway. "Ellie? Wanna go for a sleigh ride? Pa says we can hitch up the horses and pick up the Gebers and Ehrlichs and bring 'em back here for a party."

The door slammed before she could answer. She shot a questioning look at Mama and when Mama nodded she flew upstairs for warm clothes and came whirling down jabbering like Minnie.

"First time the boys ever asked *me* to go along. Emma Geber and Emma Ehrlich can come too, can't they? Can we pop corn and make hot cocoa?" Mama just sat there in the rocker looking like she was too tired to even think about it. "Mama? Can we?"

"Yes," she sighed. "I guess so. You girls will have to see that the cups are washed and . . ."

"We will! We will!"

Mama frowned. "Now, Ella, you behave yourself. You're getting to be a young lady . . . ." She cleared her throat and studied Ellen with a strange faraway look. "Yes, you *are* a young lady. A real nice looking young lady." She looked down quickly at her knitting.

Could she have heard Mama right? "A real nice looking young lady," that's what she had said all right. She wanted to hug Mama so tight but she dropped a quick kiss on her forehead instead and called, "Bye, Mama. We'll take care of everything. You just rest," as she ran out the door.

Now three hours later Ellen stood shivering by the upstairs hall window. She had loved Mama so much when she had run out with Mama's beautiful words ringing in her ears, and here she was seething with anger and resentment as the dark figures of the horses and sleigh moved slowly up the hill without her. Mama wouldn't let her go along to take the Gebers and Ehrlichs home. Mama said it was too cold—that she'd get overtired and have a sore throat. Ellen begged, pleaded and coaxed but Mama would not relent.

"She's just jealous," Ellen grumbled. "She could see what a good time I was having. I saw her frowning like everything when Bill and Henry were teasing me. Just because she never has any fun she doesn't want me to have any, either." Ellen's throat ached. She longed to cry but her tears were bottled tight in anger.

The sleigh was out of sight now, the bells silent. She shivered and tiptoed into her room and cautiously lifted the top quilt. Minnie didn't stir. She wrapped it around her and dragged it to the window overlooking the white field and the woods, beyond which the river flowed dark and still under thick ice. She strained to see the old house against the black woods where it stood ghostly quiet, its decay halted now by the cold. Poor old house. Three years since they had moved into the new home, but she still felt sad when she thought of it cold and empty and quiet.

One day last spring Ellen had seen Mama walking down the hill toward the cedar swamp and had run to join her.

"Get lonesome for the old house," Mama said as Ellen walked behind her through the cedar swamp. "Makes me mad at myself for feeling lonesome for a house. We should feel for people, not things."

Mama chatted about moving some of the rose bushes she called the "Wind Lake" roses because Papa's sister Minnie had brought them from Wind Lake years ago; they stood in the doorway looking into the shambles of their once-cozy house. "Shouldn't look at it. Makes me feel bad," Mama said and walked around the house toward the river. They looked down on the clear but copper-colored river and Mama said, "Now. Close your eyes. Think about how it looked when we lived there. Remember the calendar that always hung right above the wood box and the sewing machine under the south window and the lamp bracket by the door and the coat hooks?" They sat down in the tender spring grass and remembered and laughed and Ellen had loved Mama so much.

Now tears came and Ellen sobbed great gulping sobs into the quilt so Minnie wouldn't hear her. She hated herself for hating Mama. Mama could be so much fun— she had such good thoughts—deep thoughts—like the other day when she talked about remembering the good things and not thinking about the bad ones. Oh, how quickly she had forgotten! Of course! That was the thing to do. Remember the good things. As instantly as a lamp lighted in a dark room banishes the darkness the thought of remembering good things banished her anger. She dabbed her tears, smiled and closed her eyes . . . remembering . . . remembering. . . .

She had felt so free riding out of the driveway and heading west on the big logging sleigh. Tonight she could giggle and be silly without Mama frowning at her. She drank in great breaths of the crackling-cold air. And the sky! She could ride like this for hours with the stars hanging so low surely one could touch one at the top of the hill. Incredible to think that all those stars were there in the daytime—all the time. She had forgotten how countless they were or that the woods, so inviting by day, would look so eerie and impenetrable in the darkness.

At the crest of the maple hill Al yelled "Whoa!" and the sleigh slid to a stop. (Everyone called it "the maple hill" because two huge maple trees stood where the middle of the road should be. Papa had insisted that the road be cut on either side of them instead of cutting them down.) An icy limb cracked deep in the woods, old Nell shook her head and the sleigh bells gave a jingle and it was quiet. A silver-dipped world. Then far to the south from the heart of the timber country drifted a chorus of yips . . . then howls. Chills raced up Ellen's spine.

"Coyotes!" said Fred.

"Timber wolves!" said Al.

"You're crazy. It's coyotes."

"How would you know! Ya ain't even dry behind the ears yet!"

Fred gave Al a shove and Al pushed Fred off the sleigh into the snow. Fred came up with a clump of snow and tried to rub it on Al's face. Al plowed after Fred into the snowdrift, and the silence was broken by grunts and groans. Ellen screamed for them to stop but they paid no attention to her. Did they *have* to fight on an evening like this? Then, to her relief they sat up, laughed and climbed back on the sleigh, and they slid away down the road, the bells jingling a merry rhythm.

Freezing wind swept over Richter's clearing and Ellen snuggled deep into the hay until they turned left at the corner and she sat up to see the church steeple pierce the sky and to glance at the dark lonely school house across the road. Away they glided past Max Denker's and on to Geber's, where yellow light from the log house windows spilled out on the snow.

Emma Geber squealed with delight and ran to get heavy clothes, and Henry laced his boots, managing to keep an eye on Ellen. She ignored him and giggled with Emma, but she knew his eyes were following her.

Mrs. Geber fretted about all the noise and work they would make for Mrs. Verleger, and Ellen felt uneasy. Mrs.

Geber had never been so concerned about Mama before. The uneasy feeling soon vanished in the banter and laughter as they rode down the long winding hill and around the corner where Ehrlich's lamp-lit log house welcomed them. Bill and Emma joined them and back they went around the corner up the long winding hill, laughing and talking nonsense.

Now, standing at the window wrapped in the quilt, her face still glowed from the cold. She scratched "Henry" and "Bill" into the strip of window frost with her fingernail and then quickly melted them with the warmth of her palm. The evening was a jumble of impressions—out of sequence and incomplete. No matter. She could still feel the excitement—the dizzying realization that she was the center of both Bill's and Henry's attention. She could still see Bill's laughing face close to hers and Henry, usually so serious, jovial tonight as he shouldered Bill away and looked deep, deep into her eyes.

She pulled the quilt tighter around her and hugged herself ecstatically. Nothing like this had ever happened to her before.

Mama had a big steaming kettle of hot cocoa waiting when they got back to the house. They had warmed their hands on the hot cups and crowded around the heater stove. Papa teased the girls—telling them the horses were tired and they'd have to walk home—and Ellen had been suddenly much aware of his grimy underwear sleeves poking out of his plaid shirt cuffs. Mama, damp comb marks in her hair and wearing her best blue-flowered apron, smiled and nodded from her rocker, but Ellen knew Mama wished they'd go home so she could go to bed.

Sleepy now, Ellen laid the quilt over Minnie and groped back into her memory for the happiest possible moment to think of over and over as she undressed in the dark and cuddled close to Minnie's warm little body.

White light was seeping through the window when Papa called her Sunday morning. Everyone had slept late, but not late enough to suit Ellen.

"If I had one wish right now," she told Minnie, "it would be to stay in bed as long as I liked every single morning."

Papa would call again in a minute if he didn't hear her, so she thrust one bare foot out of bed, made a board creak and pulled it back under the covers. She *had* to think of something pleasant—something to look forward to today. Something to crowd out the angry feeling toward Mama. Papa called again.

"You didn't fool him," Minnie giggled. She grabbed her clothes and ran downstairs to dress by the oven door where it was nice and warm.

"Right now I wish I was little again," Ellen grumbled and pulled on long-legged underwear while still under the covers. She slid out of bed and exchanged her friendly nightie for an icy undershirt. "Acorns! Darn old acorns!" she growled, scowling down at the small protrusions in her undershirt. "How will I ever be able to wear ruffled blouses like Miss McKinley's? I simply have to grow a bosom! Maybe if I eat more. I'm so skinny. . . . Can't stew about that now. Got to think of something good about today—something to look forward to."

She was buttoning her shoes when she thought of it. *Time to daydream.* That was worth looking forward to. She'd work like everything and get some time for herself this afternoon and she'd crawl back in this nice warm bed and relive last night—every single good part of it!

Downstairs Mama gave the morning weather report in her usual cheerful maddening fashion, but she looked strained and pale. She's only having another baby, Ellen reminded herself. It's not like she was sick or something.

By keeping her attention on getting her work done Ellen

was able to ignore the boys' squabbling, Minnie's jabbering, Mama's scolding, Roy's whining, Gertie and John's screeching and Al and Fred's teasing. It wasn't easy.

At the breakfast table Fred nudged Al and said loud enough for Ellen to be sure to hear him. "My! My! Who ever would have thought it! Our own little sister . . ."

"If you two don't shut *up!*" she hissed.

They rolled their eyes and lifted their eyebrows. She kicked at them under the table. Fred winced. Papa gave her his you-better-stop-it-right-now frown. Mama, thank goodness, was oblivious to everything except keeping little Roy's hands out of the oatmeal bowl.

After breakfast Ellen plunged into the morning work, not even minding the overflowing slop pail, the empty water pail, slush-tracked floors, soggy roller-towel or the gray-ringed wash basin. It was the peanut shells that got her! Peanut shells on window sills, chair seats, scrunched into braided rugs and even ground to a powder in the tufts of the black leather front room couch. She swept and brushed and hollered, "The next kid I see drop a peanut shell is gonna *eat* it!"

Mamma told her to simmer down—that the shells would soon be gone along with all the rest of the Christmas disorder and a lot more Ellen didn't listen to because she was counting the minutes until dinner dishes were done and she was free.

At half past eleven the potatoes bubbled merrily and the pork roast smelled delicious.

At twelve o'clock Papa pulled his chair up under him and everyone dashed to the table.

Half past twelve Papa tilted his chair back and youngsters scattered while Ellen clattered plates into a stack.

At one o'clock—two more kettles to wash.

Sleigh bells! Dog barking. Yells. "We got company! Stuhls are here!"

Mama staggered to her feet. "Oh for goodness' sake! We don't have a thing baked but *Pfeffernuesse*. Ella, you quick stir up a molasses cake. We'll whip some cream and . . ." She looked around the room and groaned. "This house!"

Ellen echoed her groan. She was never aware of the house being shabby or disorderly until Mrs. Stuhl swept in. How she must gloat over their worn front room when she thought of her own carpeted parlor with its lace curtains, red velvet chair, fancy globe lamp with roses painted on it and lace doilies and more lace doilies. Ellen had never actually set foot in the room but she had seen it once. Not clearly because the shades were tightly drawn against a possible ray of damaging light, but she had *seen* it. Millie Stuhl had closed the door with a snug click and draped a lace-edged hankie back over the door knob so it covered the key hole. "Mama doesn't want it to get all dusty," Millie explained.

In a moment Mrs. Stuhl's eyes would sweep over these teeming rooms where each day Mama waged her valiant but futile battle against dirt and disorder. Her anger at Mama forgotten now, Ellen flew around straightening, picking up and putting away an amazing number of things that destroyed the illusion of order. She even forgot her plan to daydream. It would be fun to talk to Millie.

But Millie, who was a little older than Ellen, had stayed home to take care of baby Amanda's cold, so Ellen baked the molasses cake and listened to the grown-ups' conversation.

Clara, Walter and Ted Stuhl stared at Minnie, Ed and John—and Minnie and Ed and John stared back at them.

Mrs. Stuhl laughed and put one arm around Minnie and the other around Clara. "Go play now, children. When it's time to go home then you'll want to play."

"That's the way it goes," Mama said, suggesting they go out and coast.

It was four o'clock when Ellen poured hot water in the dishpan. "Well, wasn't that a nice visit?" Mama said, wiping the last crumbs from the table when they had gone. "Did you hear Mrs. Stuhl praise your cake, Ella?"

Ellen nodded but she didn't look particularly pleased. Mama chattered on. "Funny how I cringe when she walks in and I think of how our house must look to her, but she's so pleasant I forget all about it as soon as we start talking. I could never be that fussy about my house and she couldn't put up with our disorder but we can still be friends. Papa and Mr. Stuhl don't agree on everything either, but I'd say Ed Stuhl is Papa's best friend."

No use getting Mama riled, Ellen thought. She didn't see any sense at all in shutting the family out of a perfectly good room just so she could show off her precious parlor, but she knew there was no use arguing with Mama. It was like a tug-of-war going on in her mind. One part said, "Mama is right. Think like Mama." And the other side said, "You have a mind of your own. Believe what *you* think is right." Will one side *ever* win?

The New Year

It was good to have her hands out of the dishpan and back at her slate Monday morning. Miss McKinley spent some time talking about the new year and all the wonderful things that would happen in 1904, and told them it wouldn't be many years before they would all ride in automobiles and everyone laughed. She said in a few years electricity would do most of the work and then they really laughed. It was fun to think about, but Ellen wished there were something to do all that work right now! She didn't even want to think about all the work there would be when the new baby came. Maybe it wouldn't be so long till it came. Mama had put little Roy in the homemade bunk a long while ago, and the cradle stood empty beside Mama's bed as it always did awhile before a new baby came. Made Ellen angry just to look at it!

That night she took her time walking home from school—even played tag with Minnie and the boys. It was better than listening to Mama boss. Her mood was as dull as the gray sky. Dumb old winter. It wasn't even pretty outside anymore now that the snow by the roadside was the color of an old gray mare and the banks by the back door had disgusting yellow holes in them where the dog had gone.

She hadn't even hung up her coat when Mama said, "You change your dress and put on an apron!"

Ellen seethed. "Can't she ever give me a *chance*?" she muttered through clenched teeth and stomped upstairs and took such a long time to change Mama yelled at her to hurry up and get downstairs.

"Ellie, think we can play dominoes tonight?" Minnie asked. "You beat me last time. I want to win once. Can we?"

"Oh, Minnie. I don't *know*!"

"You promised we'd play soon. I wanna play tonight!"

"Oh, shut up, will you! I'll *see!*"

Minnie let out a wail and threw herself on the couch.

"Now what did you say to her?" Mama demanded. She looked homely when she scowled like that. "If you had half the patience that little girl has . . . oh, my goodness! Here come the men! Now you *move!*"

It wasn't enough that she had to keep jumping up to refill bowls, Gertie had to spill her milk. Ellen wanted to slap her. By the time she sat down again her food was cold. She pushed her plate away.

At least Minnie didn't jabber her head off while they did dishes. Her feelings were still hurt. Ellen was on the verge of making up with her but it was so peaceful she decided to wait 'til after dishes were done.

Mama groaned and panted around all evening and Ellen was glad to get upstairs and not have to listen to her. She tried to think of good things like Mama had said but tonight she simply wanted to be miserable. She piled grievance upon grievance until she fell asleep.

She woke with a start. It was midnight dark and the wind was moaning around the corner of the house. But there was another sound. A chill ran through her. Sobs. Deep awful sobs. Mama's sobs. She slid out of bed and ran to the top of the stairs. Papa was talking in a low steady voice but she couldn't hear what he was saying. More sobs. Papa's voice again. She stood on one foot, keeping the other one warm on top of it, then switched and stood on the other foot and wrapped her flannel night gown tight around her. Mama must have told Papa how hateful she had been tonight. What else would she be crying about? "I was horrid all evening and I didn't even say good night to her," Ellen chided herself. Mama was blowing her nose. The bed creaked and it was quiet. Quiet.

Ellen crept back to bed. "Please, God, forgive me for being so hateful and let Mama forgive me," she pleaded. She'd apologize—first thing in the morning.

Something was wrong. She knew it the moment she woke up, but it took a little while to remember what it was. Each time she recalled another detail she felt worse.

Mama was hurrying around when Ellen came downstairs. She was out of breath as usual but she wasn't looking particularly unhappy. "Sure glad that wind died down," Mama said, peering out of the east window. "We're due for more snow, though."

Whew! Mama wasn't angry anymore. Maybe she could get by just by being helpful instead of apologizing.

That evening she hurried home with good intentions that lasted almost all evening—until she was playing dominoes with Minnie and Mama told her to stop and get Gertie and Roy ready for bed.

"Can't ever satisfy her," Ellen grumbled to herself. "I play dominoes with Minnie like she wants me to and just like that—I have to stop and put kids to bed."

"What you talkin' 'bout, Ellie?" Gertie asked, lifting her pretty little face to be washed.

"Oh, nothing, honey. Sometimes I just talk to myself."

"Me too," Gertie said, ducking her head down into her shoulders with a giggle—like they shared a special secret.

Mama's prediction of more snow was right. Well, almost right. It wasn't quite cold enough Tuesday night to snow. Not until every twig was encased in a generous covering of ice did rain turn to snow and top off each intricate horizontal surface with dazzling crystals.

Papa's voice boomed over the morning commotion, "Stop and take a good look around when you go outside this morning. Nature's putting on quite a show."

On the way to school Ellen lagged behind the others. She intended to look and look and look. Just short of the maple hill she stopped and listened to the tinkle of the icy branches. Then the sun came out. She blinked back tears. Had she ever seen anything more beautiful? What did the maple trees look like? Something way back in her memory.

Reluctantly she walked away. Now she remembered! Chandeliers! Gigantic crystal chandeliers she had seen in a picture of a Viennese ballroom. She turned around and walked slowly backwards, enraptured with their splendor.

Once, walking down the street in Tomahawk, she had heard waltz music drifting out of a doorway. Papa said it was coming from a gramophone. She'd have a gramophone when she grew up. Whenever she wanted to she'd play waltz music and whirl around the house pretending it was a huge ballroom. Why, maybe someday she'd waltz in a *real* ballroom under sparkling chandeliers. She could just see it—fine ladies wearing gowns with skirts way out to here. She'd wear one exactly the same color as that sky up there.

The sun was blinding her. She turned around and

walked toward school. By the time she reached the Benson hill the ice from the trees around her began falling soundlessly into the soft snow. By evening it would all be gone.

All eyes were on her as she slid into her seat as they sang the last stanza of "My Country, 'Tis of Thee." Miss McKinley didn't look at her until they were well into "The Little Brown Church in the Wildwood" and then her glance was brief but that brief glance told Ellen, "I understand. It's *so* beautiful out there." Right then Ellen would cheerfully have died for Miss McKinley.

Mama was waiting by the south window after school. "Been watching the boys coasting on the crust. Minnie just went out. Want to run and take a ride before you take off your wraps?"

"Golly! Sure!" She shoved her lunch pail into Mama's hands, ducked under the clothesline and ran out on the icy field. Drifting snow had blown moire-like designs on the field and the low sun silvered the icy waves between the snowdrifts.

"Hey, Ellie! Come on!" Eddie yelled, looking like a little elf with his big red ears sticking out of his cap. "Wow! Does it go good!"

"You gotta stand on a strip of snow to get on or you'll take a header," Minnie called, waiting her turn while Len and George dragged the big wooden sled uphill, weaving right and left to avoid icy spots.

"Wanna go on mine?" Johnny yelled, dragging a sled just big enough for one.

"Thanks, Johnny! Guess I'll go on the big one."

George was too out of breath to talk. George always got out of breath sooner than Len.

Len turned the big wooden sled around at the top of the hill. "You girls get on and I'll kneel behind so I can help pull it back uphill."

Away they flew riding high over the deep snow—wind tearing their breaths away. Mama must have heard them scream way up in the house. Then slower and slower. They stopped as they neared the edge of the cedar swamp and tumbled off in a laughing heap.

"I never went so fast in my life," panted Ellen.

"I couldn't get my breath!" gasped Minnie.

"Ain't it swell, though?" yelled Len, scrunching his way up the hill.

Ellen made a sweeping gesture over the rolling fields. "Gee . . . you could go all over. I'd like to ride and ride but my feet are cold and I have to go in and help Mama."

In the house Ellen tugged off her mittens. "Oh, Mama, was it fun! You feel so free!"

Mama smiled and nodded. "I was watching and wishing I was right with you."

"I wish you could come out and coast. You could—sometime, couldn't you?"

"Oh, goodness no. Not at my age. What would people say if anyone saw me. Imagine! Mrs. Verleger out coasting with the kids!"

"What's the difference?" Ellen hung up her coat with a toss of her head. "I'm going to coast with my kids when I grow up no matter what anyone says."

Mama shook her head and smiled a wry smile. "Can't find enough energy to do my work let alone climb up those hills," she sighed. "But maybe *you* will. Maybe *you* will."

Moments Remembered

Before she heard Papa fix the fires Thursday morning, Ellen was awake wishing she never had to swallow again. She came downstairs with a quilt wrapped around her and huddled in a shivering lump on the oven door till Mama came out of the bedroom tying her apron strings.

"You've got a fever all right," Mama said, feeling Ellen's forehead. "Anything hurt?"

"My throat, and I ache all over," Ellen croaked.

"Oh, dear. I sure didn't want you to get sick. Gargle warm salt water and I'll get the goose grease. Nothing better than goose grease rubbed in good and covered with a nice warm woolen cloth. Minnie! Bring down Ella's pillow so she can lie right here on the couch where it's nice and warm."

Even with the little ones yelling and playing around her, Ellen slept occasionally. At noon she ate some chicken soup and drank hot tea and dozed again.

When she woke Mama looked up from the overalls she was patching and smiled—not her everyday smile—a special warm one. Mama had a way of combining a nod, a wink and a smile that made Ellen feel good all over. Ellen could count the times she had seen it, but when she did her heart felt like butter left in the warming oven.

She beamed back an equally affectionate smile.

"Feeling any better?"

Ellen nodded.

"Was hoping you'd wake up. Gets lonesome with no one to talk to but the little ones." She gestured toward the bedroom. "They're sound asleep." She bit off the thread and held the needle toward the light to rethread it.

"Just think. If we were rich you'd never have to patch overalls. Wouldn't you like to be rich?"

"Can't say I'd miss patching overalls, but I wouldn't like to be rich."

Ellen sat up so fast her head spun. "You wouldn't want to be rich?"

"Oh, I wouldn't mind having more money so you children could go on to school if you wanted to, and we do need a bigger house already, and it would be nice to have an organ so you girls could learn to play—but don't ever think that money alone makes people happy. It takes a lot more than that." She shook the needle at Ellen. "Look at the people who jump out of windows or shoot each other. Those people aren't all poor, you know."

"I s'pose not. But did you ever really know any rich people?"

"Can't say I have. What I learned about them was from reading and from your Aunt Gustie—Papa's sister Gustie, not mine. She worked for wealthy people in Milwaukee." Mama clucked her tongue. "The things she used to tell us! Those people have trouble we don't even know about. Another thing, don't ever think all rich people are hard

58

working or smarter than poor people. A good many of them didn't do a thing but get born into the rich families while other folks work hard all their lives and never get rich."

"Do you really mean you'd rather be the way we are now than have people do your work and lots of money?"

"I told you," Mama said, sounding a little aggravated, "I'm happy being me—right here—right now." She put her patching aside and stuck wood in both stoves. "Want some tea? The *Kaffee Kuchen* is cool."

"My stomach says 'yes' but my throat says 'no.'" Ellen grinned. "My stomach just won."

Cuddled in Mama's old flannel wrapper, Ellen watched Mama slice fresh cinnamon-topped *Kaffee Kuchen* and pour tea. "Tell me about when you were a little girl and lived in Oshkosh."

"Well, I don't remember so much when we lived there but I remember getting off the train when we came from Oshkosh. I remember walking on a board sidewalk in Ogema. I was ten, you know. I didn't know my pa and wouldn't let him help me off the train because he had grown a beard. He'd been up here working in the woods— took him three weeks with the oxen. Well, we walked out to where my brother Walter lives now—about ten miles from Ogema. Stayed in a house up on Ring's hill that night and walked the rest of the way the next day. Many's the time I walked that ten miles and back in one day."

"Tell me about the Indians."

"Well, my brothers and I ran ahead down the road— more like a trail it was—and ran headlong into two Indians. We came back running for dear life hollering—in German of course—'the devils are after us!' Ma said we scared those poor Indians more than they scared us."

"Did they really look fierce?"

"Shucks, no. Just strange."

"Did they wear buckskin clothes and feathers?"

Mama laughed. "Heavens, no. They wore the same kind of clothes the lumberjacks wore in those days, but their faces were dark brown and they had high cheekbones."

"I thought Indians were red."

"Ones I seen looked dark brown to me."

"But what do you remember about Oshkosh?"

"Mostly I remember peddling truck vegetables Ma raised. Didn't bother me any but you should have heard my sister Winnie—you know Aunt Winnie who lives out in Knox Mills. She hated selling vegetables something awful. My brothers would say, 'Ah, yes. Winnie will get married and have a big garden and she'll wheel her cart down the street and yell *Knoblauch* and *Sellerie* and *Kartoffel*'—that's garlic and celery and potatoes. Oh, how she used to bawl. One time I got in trouble, though. Someone had painted a stairs and put a board across it. Didn't I go and take that board down and come tromping up those wet stairs. That lady didn't buy any vegetables that day!"

"What else did you do?"

"We played down by Lake Winnebago, I remember. Never did learn to swim. Gustie did, though. There wasn't much Gustie didn't try."

"That's the Aunt Gustie who lives in Ashland?"

Mama nodded. "Miss Gustie. You'd like her." Mama's eyes twinkled and she shook her head. "Wonder if she's still so full of the dickens."

"You had a sister Anne too, didn't you?"

"Yes, she died when I was sixteen—left little Anne, you know. Anne lived with my folks till they died and then she went to live with Clara and Walter. Seemed more like a sister to me than a niece. My! The hours I used to sing and waltz with her in my arms to keep her from crying."

Ellen giggled. "I'd like to see you waltz with her in your arms now. She's bigger than you are."

Mama clapped her hands. "Ach! Look who woke up!"

John padded out on stocking feet, head down, and hid his face in Mama's apron. She patted his back. "You feel like I do when I wake up from a nap. Takes a little while to figure out what's going on. Nice fresh *Kuchen*! Want some?"

John scrambled up on the bench grinning above his deep-dimpled chin that was so much like Papa's.

"You'd better lie down again, Ella. Later if you feel like it I'd like you to peel potatoes."

It felt good to lie down again but best of all it felt good to be at peace with Mama. It was so nice when they could talk like friends. But Mama just couldn't mean what she said about not wanting to be rich, could she? Ellen tried to imagine Mama wearing elegant clothes and it made her smile to think about it. Mama wouldn't even wear a bright-colored apron because Papa didn't like her to wear bright colors. Then she imagined Mama seated at a china, crystal and silver-laden table. She'd be dismayed by all the unfamiliar dishes. What would she do? Blunder along hoping she wouldn't do something wrong? Not Mama! She'd lean toward someone near her and whisper, "This is all new to me. I don't know what to use first. Do you mind if I watch what you do?" Chances are that person would be as helpful and gracious as the store clerks Mama often questioned. It was so embarrassing when Mama asked questions in stores and didn't even pretend to know things. Once she asked Mama why she didn't make-believe she knew things, and Mama said she'd never learn anything that way and that there was no disgrace in not knowing everything. "It's just a matter of where you live," she said. "Do you suppose city ladies know all about farm things? Think a minute. If a city lady came here and pretended to know everything about the farm, sooner or later she'd make a mistake and look mighty foolish. But, if she came

61

and admitted that she knew very little about farm life you'd be glad to help her, wouldn't you? Another thing," Mama had leaned forward in a confidential manner, "people like to be asked advice. It makes them feel worthwhile."

Ellen wiggled into a more comfortable position on the couch. It sounded right, the way Mama explained it, but Ellen still felt it was safer to pretend. It would be just terrible to be snubbed.

Ellen felt terrible right now. Her throat hurt, her head ached and her eyes burned. It wasn't fun to lie here and watch Mama waddle around instead of helping her, either. Wonder why Mama's feet are so fat all of a sudden? she thought. They bulged out of her house slippers. The last few days her face looked puffy, too, and her eyes looked sort of pink-rimmed. All on account of that baby!

After supper Papa told Fred to stay in and help Minnie with dishes instead of doing chores, and Ellen was thankful to crawl off to bed.

The next morning Ellen's throat felt like it was so dry it would break. She reached for the glass of water she had brought up the night before. It was frozen solid. She tried to go back to sleep but her throat was so dry she got up and went downstairs. Everyone was eating breakfast. She ate a little corn mush with cold milk and cuddled in a fluffy quilt on the couch.

Mama was trying to iron when Ellen woke up an hour later, but she had to sit down every few minutes.

"I'll iron awhile," Ellen said, taking the iron from Mama's hand. "I feel lots better than I did this morning."

"All right," Mama sighed. She felt Ellen's forehead. "No fever today. Better gargle some hot salt water, though."

Ellen gargled and spat in the ugly old slop pail. How did Mama stand to see nothing but this ugly pail, wet socks, soggy mittens, chips and ashes around the stoves, and tracked floors? What was there besides dirt and ashes to see, and what did she do besides work, work, work?

"Mama, don't you get tired of work and dirt day after day?"

"Sure do, but I try not to think about the unpleasant things. I think about how much Papa and you children need things done and how glad I am to be able to do them." She poured heavy cream into the churn. "I tell myself how good I've got it in here by the nice warm fire instead of out there in that freezing woods." She chuckled and lowered her voice like she was telling a secret. "I'm getting to be a regular old house cat this winter. Don't even want to go out and empty the pot, but I do it because I hate to have the boys do it."

"I have to get ours down and let it thaw out before I can empty it." Ellen giggled. "Isn't it funny, no matter when I take out that old pot I'm sure to meet one of the boys head on in the doorway."

Mama stopped churning a moment. "Isn't it silly? A person shouldn't be embarrassed—everyone has to go— it's just the way we've always been. We all act like nobody else does such things."

Gertie heard them laughing and came running. "What you laughin' at?" she demanded, yanking at Mama's skirt.

"Oh, just something silly," Mama said, smoothing her shiny blonde hair. "You've been playing so nicely this morning maybe Ella can find some raisins for you and you can have a little party with John and Roy."

Mama poured off the buttermilk. "Want some, Ella?"

Ellen handed Gertie some raisins and she let out a whoop and ran into the front room. The buttermilk felt good on Ellen's raw throat.

Mama sat down with a big bowl of butter on her lap and worked the butter to one side of the bowl and then the other with a wooden paddle to get out every drop of buttermilk. She glanced out the window over the snow-covered fields crisscrossed with sled tracks and footprints.

Ellen followed her glance. "Won't it be nice when spring comes? Wish I was walking down by the river right now."

Mama nodded. "I miss the river. Wish we could have moved it right up here by the road. Oh dear, I'll never forget how nice that river sounded the first night when we came back from living in Phillips."

"How come you came back?"

"It didn't work out at all the way we thought it would. We figured we'd be able to save a lot of money." Mama gave a wry laugh. "Papa had all he could do to earn enough for a roof over our heads and food, so we came back even if it was terribly hard to live without money. The only money we had was when the logs were sold once a year—unless Papa sold a little butter or some meat in Tomahawk. We had enough work, all right. No end of it—but even though we raised most of our food there were still shoes and clothes and tools and salt and sugar and flour to buy." She clucked her tongue. "That next sack of flour. That was always the homesteader's big worry."

"Why do you always say 'homestead' instead of just farm?"

"Because these are homesteads. Way back in 1860 the Homestead Act was passed that allowed people to claim a quarter section of land—that's a hundred and sixty acres —and start farming it. When they had buildings on it and land under plow a couple years later they went and 'proved up' and paid a small fee, and the land was deeded to them free and clear. Ask Papa to show you our deed. It's signed by President Harrison himself!"

"You mean they *gave* land away?"

"Don't know how else the land would have got settled. People had all they could do to buy a few head of stock, some tools, nails and window glass without paying for land."

"Gee, that was a good law."

"Yes and no. Someone can always manage to spoil any good law. Around here some men made out to be homesteading, but all they did was log off all the good timber on their own section and all the sections around as well and move on without ever proving up—just left the cutover land lie there for someone else." She stood up and patted the butter into gray earthenware crocks. "Never want you to feel like you aren't as good as rich folks," she said with bitterness in her voice. "A lot of them got rich logging land that wasn't theirs."

The clock struck eleven with heavy leaden tones. "My land!" Mama exclaimed. "Where did the forenoon go?"

After dinner Ellen rested and Mama napped awhile and then tackled a pile of darning.

Ellen sat up when she saw Mama.

"Can I help darn socks?"

"Well, I'd rather have you wind a skein of yarn if you don't mind standing. There's a skein upstairs by the spinning wheel that I washed but didn't get wound."

Upstairs in the hallway Ellen idly turned the wheel remembering how it sounded when Mama spun. Papa didn't like to hear the thunk, thunk, thunk of the spinning wheel in the evening so Mama did the spinning during the day. It was fun to watch Mama spin yarn, but even more fun to watch her twist several strands together. Mama would slip several spools—sometimes three, sometimes four, on a stout wire, fit the wire into holes in a cardboard box, pick up all the ends of yarn and attach them to an empty spool on the spinning wheel, give the wheel a spin—the opposite direction from the way it turned when she spun—and away it went on and on and on until the spool was full. So effortless compared to the stop and start of spinning when the fibers ran out, or a fluffy-carded roll was used up, or when the carpet-warp string belt flew off again and again. Mama'd get so disgusted when that belt kept flying off. All she ever said was "shucks" or "darn" but Ellen suspected Mama *thought* some other words!

"Remember when I was so short I had to run around the chairs to wind yarn instead of reaching over the back?" Ellen said as she set two chairs back to back and stretched the skein of yarn over them.

"That doesn't seem very long ago. You've really grown these past two years."

"I'm five foot five inches. How tall are you, Mama?"

"That's what I used to be but I suppose I'm shorter now because I'm getting round-shouldered."

"What makes people round-shouldered?"

"Oh, I suppose it comes from not standing and sitting straight but it could be inherited. My mother was round-shouldered as long as I can remember her."

"The only thing I remember about Grandma Kamin is one time we went to visit her and she pulled a crumpled bag of peppermints out from under her mattress and gave me some."

"Guess that's where I get my taste for peppermint," Mama said, rolling up a pair of socks and reaching for another one. "Do you remember when she did all her work resting her knee on that low chair? She never put weight on that leg for at least seven years—not that anyone saw at least—and then just like that one day she set it aside and walked on that leg the rest of her life!"

"Why did she walk on it all of a sudden?"

Mama shrugged. "I don't know. Ma was odd. We just let her alone and no one said a thing about it."

"Mama? You won't be mad if I tell you something?"

"Well, I'll try not to be but I can't really promise."

Ellen's eyes stayed on the yarn she was winding. "I still feel terrible about it . . . the day Papa stopped at school and told us Grandma Kamin had died I didn't feel sad at all. I thought, 'I better cry or the kids will think I'm awful.' I looked in the mirror out in the coatroom and told myself, 'Your grandma just died. Your grandma just died,' and tried to squeeze out a few tears. Wasn't that terrible?"

Mama smiled. "No, that wasn't terrible. You never really knew her. How could you feel sad? Glad you told me 'cause I don't want you to feel bad about it any more."

Ellen smiled at Mama, feeling all warm and loving but a little embarrassed. "Do you think she was afraid to die?" she said quickly.

"No, I don't think so. She believed in God. I think she was ready to go."

"I don't think I'll ever be ready to die," Ellen said with a little shiver. "Doesn't it scare you when you think about it?"

"Yes," Mama said, rocking gently with the darning lying idle in her lap. "There were times I was afraid to die. It's scary to think of doing something no one knows anything about—and doing it alone. Then I got to thinking, 'Isn't a person foolish to think that way? God says He's always with us.' I think we'll be with God right away when we die."

"If I was as good as you maybe I wouldn't be scared either."

Mama stopped rocking abruptly. "You know better than that. It's not how good you are that counts—it's your faith that Christ died to save you."

"But the Bible does say that faith without works is dead . . ."

"Yes, but it's still faith that makes us want to do God's will because we love God, not that we're trying to work our way to heaven. My land! How did we get into such a serious conversation?"

"We were talking about Grandma."

Mama sighed. "I miss her. Not like those first years after I got married, though. I'd get so lonesome I just had to see her. I'd take little Al and Fred and walk through the woods—must be a good four miles. Coming home I'd have to carry Fred and I'd tell myself I'd never do that again but one nice day away I'd go. You know people didn't think anything of walking miles and miles. Your Papa and I walked to Ogema and back to get married— that's about thirteen miles one way.

"How did you meet Papa? You never told me."

"Oh, he had been around this country several years. 'Big Al' the men called him. Worked with a surveying crew some of the time and in the woods, of course. He walked so fast, it was said, that his coat tails stood straight out behind him. He got along good with the young people— played accordion for dances."

"Wasn't it thrilling when Papa courted you?"

Mama laughed. "It wasn't like the courting you read about. Things were pretty matter-of-fact. Lumberjacks wanted wives, and the girls wanted husbands and none of us had a lot of people to choose from." Mama leaned back with a serene smile on her face. "We've been happy. Real happy. Your papa's the best man I ever knew." She sat up straight and picked up her darning. "He don't make a lot of fuss but he feels real deep."

Ellen frowned. It didn't sound like much fun. She wound a little faster. Her legs didn't feel like standing. "What was the happiest day of your life, Mama?"

"That would be hard to say. I've had a great many happy days. Like the day Ma said we weren't going back to Oshkosh. We only came to visit Pa, but when Ma saw what nice *Kartoffel* and *Mangle-Worzel* we could grow

68

here, she changed her mind. Well, that day we kids ran outside whooping and hollering we were so happy. Poor Ma. I think she cried half the winter, she was so lonesome for her sister and her friends. At least she knew where Pa was, though. He couldn't run off with the German band like he did in Oshkosh."

"Grandpa fought in the Civil War, didn't he?"

"Lost his right eye, he did! Hardly got over here from Hanover and they drafted him."

"They weren't married then, were they?"

"Oh, yes. My oldest brother, Fred, was born in Hanover. My mother came from Braunschweig—you remember so you can tell your children someday."

"This must be family-history day," Ellen said as the last round of yarn slipped from the chair and the ball ate it up.

"Good girl! Now I'll have enough yarn for awhile. Better put wood in the stoves. I was thinking I'd better wash my hair. You feel like helping me?"

Ellen always enjoyed helping Mama wash her hair. She'd brush it and wave it around her face and Mama would look so pretty. Mama'd tolerate her fussing just so long and then she'd grab the comb, bundle it into one long rope, twist it tight and wrap it back into a pug. Today Ellen didn't try to wave it. Not even wavy hair would make Mama look pretty these days.

Ellen was pouring pitchers of water over Mama's head when Gertie came into the kitchen—nose twitching.

"I smell somethin'!"

"You smell the vinegar in the rinse water. Vinegar takes all the soap out and makes the hair shine," Ellen explained.

Gertie put her fat little hand over her mouth and giggled. Mama looked so funny with her hair hanging down all messed up. She ran to tell John.

"Mama's getting gray!" Ellen teased.

"Well, I'm thirty-five. Should have a few gray hairs by now."

The clock struck four. Ellen grimaced. In a little while the boys and Minnie would charge in and destroy this peaceful clock-ticking, fire-snapping afternoon. Mama would yell and scold and look like she couldn't keep going one more minute.

How right she was. When the school children dashed in the atmosphere of the house changed as abruptly as when a sudden summer storm sweeps the calm of a sunny day into dusty whirls, sends tin pails rattling across the yard, and ruffles the feathers of indignant hens. Ellen gritted her teeth. There'd be no end to this storm till bedtime.

After supper, Papa pushed back his chair and lit his pipe. Mama began setting dishes together—still seated.

"Emma! What's this?" Papa caught her left hand.

Mama tried to pull her hand away and then let it go limp in his grasp. "You mean my wedding ring? I—I just put it on my ring finger the other day. It fits fine now."

Mama had always worn her plain gold band on her middle finger because it was too large for her ring finger. Papa's sister Gustie had bought it for him in Milwaukee. Papa wanted to have it made smaller, but Mama didn't want to part with it, so she always wore it on her middle finger.

"You know I don't mean your ring! Look at your hands! How long have they been swollen like this?" His expression softened as Mama's chin crumpled. He let her hand slip away as she pulled herself to her feet and waddled toward the bedroom.

All eyes were on Papa's frowning face. "You boys get at chores—except you, Fred. You stay in and help with dishes." He followed Mama and shut the bedroom door behind him.

A few minutes later he came out, still frowning, pulled

on his coat and went out without a word. The only sound was the clink of the dishes and the slosh of water.

Mama came out and sat in the rocker, her eyes red and her face blotchy. She beckoned to Ellen, and Ellen sat down beside her.

"Ella? How do you feel?"

"I'm all right, Mama. I haven't had a fever all day."

Mama closed her eyes and leaned her head against the high back of the rocker. "Thank goodness you're better. Now you listen close. We're not going to do one thing that isn't necessary. The main thing is to keep everyone fed and to take care of the little ones. Papa says I am to stay in bed." Her lip trembled and she got up as quickly as she could manage and went into her bedroom.

Fred's eyes mirrored Ellen's fear but he shrugged and said, "Probably something she ate. She'll be all right in a day or two."

Oh, no! Oh, no! She couldn't laugh—she'd never stop. If only she could talk to Fred about the baby—he must know. But she simply could not bring herself to talk to him about Mama having a baby!

As soon as the evening work was done and the little ones were in bed, Ellen dragged herself upstairs, wishing she just felt half as well as she had pretended to feel. She tried to pray—to ask God to make Mama well, but her angry feeling about the baby crowded out her prayers. She hated that baby—no, she couldn't ever hate a real baby— not a baby with a face all its own—but this wasn't really a baby yet. It was just something that kept Mama sick. "Oh, just hurry up and get here," she muttered, "so we can all get back to *living* again."

The Doctor Arrives

The night Papa told Mama she should stay in bed, Ellen twisted and moaned through cycles of dreaming and waking with her predominating emotion one of anger toward the creature housed in Mama's body—the cause of it all. She'd shake herself awake, assure herself she was dreaming and dream it all again.

Morning found her dreading the coming day, but when she smelled the match sulfur and Papa's pipe smoke drifting up the stairway, she dressed quickly and hurried down to start cooking breakfast. She'd take Mama's breakfast to her. Imagine Mama having breakfast in bed. What fun! She'd use the cup and saucer with the roses and put thick cream on Mama's oatmeal and boil an egg. Mama hated fried eggs. She said she had fried so many eggs in her lifetime she could hardly stand to look at one much less eat it.

The big boys came down, still half asleep, and went out

to do chores. "Don't slam the door," Ellen warned.

She heard the heater stove door open and looked around the doorway. There stood Mama, fully dressed, putting wood in the stove.

"Oh, Mama, I was going to bring you breakfast in bed!"

"Oh, for goodness' sakes. Such nonsense. I'm feeling better this morning. I'll just help a little bit and then I'll lie down again. Here, put the breadboard over here and I'll slice the bread."

Ellen put the board down none too gently and plunked the loaf of bread beside it. Mama *would* have to spoil her plans!

Mama sliced two slices and laid down the knife. "Oh, dear, I'm not feeling as well as I thought I was. Think you can manage? I'll just sit here in the rocker and boss. I would like a cup of coffee when you have time."

Ellen's face brightened as she took the egg out of boiling water and poured coffee into the cup with the roses and finished Mama's tray.

Mama was leaning back with her eyes closed.

"Mama?"

She sat up quickly. "Well now, doesn't that look good!" She smiled her thanks.

Amply rewarded, Ellen scurried around making breakfast for everyone else. The men came in before she had things ready. The little ones woke up and she had to dress little Roy and stop Gertie and John's fights, and she knew Mama was tense because things weren't ready, and she knew she had boiled the coffee too long, and the oatmeal was lumpy, and she felt dizzy and hungry and she wished she could run upstairs and crawl back in bed and stay there all day.

After breakfast dishes were done and she was kneading bread, she felt better. It was fun to knead bread, although it wasn't as simple as it looked when Mama did it. What a sticky mess it was until she had worked in enough flour to be able to give the big tin pan a quarter turn as she kneaded . . . one, two, three, turn! One, two, three, turn! Now she was doing it. The smooth warm bulk of it had a comforting feel to it and she kneaded on and on.

"My land, you've kneaded that enough," Mama called from where she was lying on the couch. "Let it rise now."

Reluctantly she buttered the big gray bowl, plopped the dough in it and turned it over buttered side up as she had seen Mama do it so many times.

"Cover it with a clean dish towel and set it on the reservoir," Mama directed—as if Ellen didn't know.

The day hung on tightwire tension. It bothered Ellen to see Papa come in every little while—once for dry mittens, once with an armload of wood (Papa rarely carried wood and the boxes were both full), once for matches and so on. He'd shoot a questioning glance at Mama lying on the couch, and she'd return a wan smile and he'd go out again. Ellen was glad when Mama went to bed and stayed there most of the afternoon. Papa drove to Ogema with the team and sleigh and brought home groceries—and white peppermint candies for Mama with little x's on them, and chocolate drops for everyone else.

By evening the bread, fragrant and crusty brown, was cooling on the table. "It's the only thing I can see that I've done all day," Ellen mumbled to herself. At supper her face flushed when Papa said, "Good bread, Ellie. Never tasted better!" Later, in bed, aching tired, she clung to those words like a comforting blanket and slept from sheer exhaustion.

Sunday morning she felt strong and eager to tackle the task of running the household. Why, she felt positively grown up!

By evening she felt not so grown up—and wished she was a little girl again.

Mama had stayed in her room all day and didn't seem to care what Ellen cooked when she asked her what to have for meals. Papa went in and out peeking at Mama, and occasionally talking with her.

When the little ones woke up from their naps, Papa sat in the rocker and held Gertie and Roy and sang in a deep soft voice snatches of little German tunes and then hummed "Rock of Ages." Ellen stole glances at him hoping to see him smile. He never did.

Tense with concern, but physically exhausted, Ellen went to bed and slept soundly.

Very early in the morning she heard Papa put wood in the stoves and went back to sleep so soundly that she didn't hear him come up the stairs and into the room. She let out a little cry when he gave her shoulder a gentle shake.

"Sh! Don't wake Minnie. Thought I better wake you early. Come right down."

Papa was lacing his boots and didn't look up when she came down. She huddled over the stove, sensing Papa had something to tell her.

Still looking at his boots he said, "Your ma's awful sick. Mrs. Geber's been here since about midnight. I sent word for Dr. Pearson to come when I went to Ogema Saturday. He ought to be here today. You get going now and get breakfast and pack lunches." He closed the door quietly behind him—never once meeting Ellen's eyes.

Al and Fred came down slit-eyed and tousle-haired.

Ellen stood shivering by the stove—fist pressed tight against her lips.

"What's ailin' you?" Fred asked, smothering a yawn.

"Mama's awful sick. The *doctor's* coming," she whispered.

Fred's eyes flew open. "Gee whiz! A real doctor!"

Ellen nodded and blinked back tears. "We never had a

doctor—not even when Ed was so sick when we lived in the old house that Mama and Mrs. Geber were crying 'cause they thought he was gonna die."

Al nodded. "Yeah. I remember . . ."

"Wow!" Fred said looking pale. "You think . . .?"

"Aw, don't worry, she's just having a baby," Al cut in. "Mrs. Geber's getting old. Probably don't want to deliver babies alone anymore. Lots of people have doctors deliver babies."

"Like who, smarty?" Ellen challenged. "Name someone around here!"

"Now, Ellie, Al's right. Times are changing, you know."

"Well, I'm scared!" Ellen's voice broke.

"Well, I'm hungry. Get moving, will ya?" Al said roughly.

Fred began to protest and Ellen turned just in time to see Al raise his eyebrows at Fred. Fred gulped and headed out the door. The boys were as scared as she was. She just *knew* it.

Teeth chattering, she put water on to boil for coffee and oatmeal, sliced bread, set table and began to make lunch.

Mrs. Geber came out and offered to stir the oatmeal while Ellen ran upstairs to get little Roy, who woke up crying and frightened because he didn't remember Papa carrying him up there during the night. Mrs. Geber sat down a few minutes and drank a cup of coffee, but she didn't talk about Mama, and Ellen didn't dare ask her.

After the children left for school and Ellen was washing dishes, Mrs. Geber came out again. "Your Ma wants to talk to you, Ellen."

Mama was lying with her eyes closed. Except for the dark rings under her eyes, her face was almost as white as the pillow case. Ellen's heart thumped so loud she was afraid Mama would hear it.

"Mama?" she whispered.

Mama's eyelids trembled but she didn't open her eyes. "Ella . . . you'll just have to stay home. Can't be helped. Get the boys to help you . . ." Her jaw relaxed and her mouth hung open. Mrs. Geber put her arm around Ellen's shoulders and eased her from the room. Mrs. Geber tried to say something but no words came. She shook her head and turned away but not quickly enough to hide her tears.

Ellen fled to the pantry and sobbed over the flour barrel. "Oh, please, God! Let her be all right!"

"Ellie?" Fred called softly. "Pa says I should help you in here."

She dried her eyes on her apron and came out, but as soon as she tried to talk she began to cry again. "I—I saw her. She's white as the pillow case and Mrs. Geber was *crying.*"

"Hey! Cut it out. You'll get the little ones upset and then you'll really have something," Fred warned, awkwardly patting her arm.

A tear hissed on the hot stove as Ellen went back to work. "How would it be if you took the little ones for a long sleigh ride? It's sunny and not too cold and no wind . . ."

"Pa said I'm supposed to help you."

"You think that ain't helping?"

Fred grinned. "Uh, sure. I guess so. You gotta get 'em dressed, though."

Fred and the little ones had disappeared below the east hill when the doctor's cutter came from the west.

Papa met the doctor in the yard, talked briefly and began unhitching the doctor's horses. The doctor took his black bag out of the buggy and walked toward the house.

Ellen stepped back from where she had been watching by the window, bit her lip and straightened her apron. What should she say? She had never seen a doctor before. She waited until he knocked and hastily opened the door.

"How-do, young lady," he said, nodding to her like she was a grown-up woman. She immediately felt at ease. He seemed so small compared to Papa, and he had red hair and freckles and his skin looked oddly soft. She took his coat and ran to lay out a clean towel when he asked where he could wash.

He rolled back his starched white cuffs, soaped his arms and hands, rinsed them and then poured some vile-smelling liquid over them, ignored the towel and dried them over the stove. Papa came in as he was drying his hands. He gestured to Papa to bring his bag and he followed Papa to the bedroom. The door closed behind them with a firm click.

If only her knees would stop trembling. Ellen tried to work but she kept listening . . . listening for that first little cry. "Got to relax. The doctor knows what to do. Soon it will all be over," she told herself.

She watered Mama's geraniums, picked off a dry leaf and stood staring out of the east window. In a little while . . . in a little while all the wondering and waiting and anger would be forgotten. The baby would soon be old enough to gurgle and coo and welcome her home each night with a smile and outstretched arms. It would be fun to watch the baby learn all the cunning little things Roy and all the babies before him had learned. And Mama'd be strong and sing as she worked again. Her legs felt stronger now and she smiled. Someday when the baby was grown up maybe she'd tell him all about it—how angry she was about its coming, and they'd laugh. She tried to picture it. Maybe it would be a flaxen haired little girl like Gertie instead of another dimple-chinned boy. It would be nice to have another sister. But that didn't matter—like Mama always said, "Just so it's a healthy baby."

"Well, little baby," she said to herself, "someday I'll tell you just what it was like the day you were born. It was during a January thaw," I'll say. "A clear blue day it was that smelled like spring out on the well platform where the boards steamed in the sun. Icicles dripped, dripped, dripped from the roof, and now and then a chunk of ice and snow slid off the roof with a grating sound followed by a crash. Way up the hill where Fred was pulling the little ones on the big sled the sleigh tracks glinted in the sun. A dozen or so plump chickadees pecked at the dog dish on the stoop and ignored the sleeping dog beside it." Ellen turned and looked around the room, blinking her eyes to help them adjust from the bright outdoor light. "I'll tell you all about this house. About the big black stove with 'Home Comfort' in shiny nickel-plated letters on the oven door—about the stag in a woods etched in the glass of the front door. And I'll tell you how proud and happy Papa looked when he told me you had been born. And Mama—how her face sort of glowed when she held you. Yes, little baby, I'll tell you just how it was and I'll tell you too that even though I wasn't a bit happy to know you were coming, that before you were born that day I knew I loved you."

Enough dreaming. Better sweep the floor while everyone was outside. Ears tuned to hear the first cry, she worked quietly. Occasionally she heard a mumble of voices. She leaned on the broom handle, cheek on hand. She could just feel that downy little head indescribably soft against her lips—and those tiny fingers would grasp her thumb so amazingly tight. It would make contented little sounds at Mama's breast and then loll its sleepy head on Mama's arm. Little Roy would point and squeal at the strange wiggly little creature, and the big boys would talk to it when no one was watching—and Minnie! Minnie would love it and love it and love it!

She distinctly heard Mama moan. Her pulse raced. What would she do if Mama really cried out? Could she stand to hear it? What if the little ones came back in and heard her? She began to tremble again.

Thung! The clock struck half past eleven.

Papa came out of Mama's room but he didn't say a word—didn't even look at her. He put on his coat and went out. She heard pounding and sawing in the shed.

Mama didn't moan again but she heard the doctor's voice and now and then Mrs. Geber's.

"Sh!" she cautioned Fred when he brought the little ones in. He helped undress the runny-nosed, red-cheeked little ones while Gertie and John jabbered and little Roy cried because he was cold and hungry.

"They'll take good naps," she assured Fred while she fed little Roy.

Papa and Al came in, washed and sat down at the table. Al ate but Papa only drank coffee.

"Fred, you better help Al this afternoon and get those wood boxes filled before you go out to feed."

Tense, ears straining, Ellen washed dishes when the little ones were asleep upstairs.

Mrs. Geber came out and got a basin of water and went back to Mama's room. All she said was, "Keep those fires burning."

What was taking so long? Papa had gone back to Mama's room after dinner, too. About one he came out and told Ellen to fix something for the doctor to eat. He sat down in the rocker and lit his pipe. "I'll have coffee with him," he said, and Ellen waited for him to say more. He only rocked and smoked and stared at the heater stove door.

She set two places, using saucers like Mama always did, for company. When everything was ready and the doctor hadn't come out Ellen took the spoons out of the spoon-holder, washed and dried it, and put the spoons back, carefully polishing each one.

He came out before she finished, washed his hands again—this time drying them on the clean towel, rolled down his sleeves, buttoned his cuffs and sat down.

"You say you have ten children, Mr. Verleger?"

Papa stirred his coffee and nodded.

"Nice family. Real nice family."

Ellen poured more coffee. What did he mean, ten children? *What about the baby?* She tried not to stare at his soft white hands. They looked more like a woman's hands.

Dr. Pearson ate hungrily and talked about a terrible fire in the Iroquois Theater in Chicago where hundreds of people had been killed. Ellen shuddered. Papa seemed unaffected. He just stirred his coffee round and round. Something *was* wrong! Ordinarily Papa would be laughing and talking a blue streak. He loved to talk with people.

Al came in.

"Get the doctor's horses ready," Papa said, and Al slipped out again.

Dr. Pearson got up. "Well, I'll have another look at Mrs. Verleger," he said. He came out frowning and accepted his coat from Papa. "Sure wish there were more I could do, Mr. Verleger," he said, shaking his head. He turned to Ellen. "Good-bye, young lady. Your pa's mighty lucky to have a capable daughter like you."

He was gone before she could reply.

Not one word about the baby. Ellen's stomach felt sick.

Papa went out with the doctor and in a few minutes he came back in and stood by the kitchen stove and rubbed his hands over the stove making a chalk-dry sound.

"Ellie?"

She was at his side.

He cleared his throat. "Guess you knew there was a baby expected." He looked sideways at her as she nodded. He took a deep breath and Ellen held hers. "Was afraid

82

something was wrong when your Ma swelled up like that. The baby came awhile ago. It was dead."

Ellen let out a little cry and bit her knuckle hard.

"Worst part of it is," Papa swallowed and blinked his eyes, "your Ma's awful sick."

Thoughts tumbled in on each other—battered her like hail. *There's no baby! I got my wish!* I *wanted* something to happen to it. Babies are too much work. I *wanted* it to happen! The baby is dead and *it's all my fault.* Ellen sobbed loudly.

Papa's face loomed close to hers—his jaws clenched, eyes blazing. He shook her by the shoulders. "Stop it, Ella! You want her to hear you?"

She struggled to obey, choking back the sobs. Papa drew her close against his rough wool coat and patted her back with his big calloused hand.

She pulled away. "Was it a boy or a girl?" she whispered.

"A boy."

"Oh, Papa," she sobbed again against his coat. "It's all my fault."

"What on earth are you talking about—all your fault?"

What was the use? How could she ever explain how she had wished the baby just wouldn't *be.* Papa would hate her. He couldn't help hate her. She couldn't tell him—not now! She cried a little longer against his shoulder, then pulled away and blew her nose. "What will we do?"

Papa wiped his eyes on the back of his hand, then pulled out a big red handkerchief and gave a loud blow. "You'll have to do most of the housework and help take care of your ma. Mrs. Geber'll help. Right now I want you to go upstairs and see that the little ones don't come down for awhile. We won't tell the children anything except that Ma's sick. I'll tell the big boys about . . ." He nodded toward Mama's room.

Huddled against the warm chimney in the upstairs hallway, she heard Papa go out, come in again, and Mama's door open and close. She tiptoed to the south window of her room where Gertie, John and Roy lay sleeping and looked out across the field, over the cedar swamp to the old house. She heard Papa walk through the house and close the door softly. He headed toward the barn carrying something in front of him. As he turned left at the well platform she saw it—a box about two feet long made of bright new lumber.

"Papa! Oh, Papa!" She fled to the big boys' room so she wouldn't wake the little ones and sobbed into a pillow that smelled like hair tonic. Why, there must be four feet of snow out there—and another three feet of frozen ground to dig through. "Oh, little baby! Poor little baby. I'm so sorry—so sorry." Such a little while ago she had been able to almost feel that warm soft little head against her cheek. Had Mama been thinking how it would feel to hold a new little one? *Mama!* She had to see her. She blew her nose, dabbed her eyes and rushed downstairs.

Mrs. Geber sat at the table, head in her hands, looking tired enough to die.

"Can I get you something to eat?"

"A little bread and butter, maybe. And coffee, please."

Ellen poured coffee and Mrs. Geber took a loud sip. "Your pa—he told you about the baby?"

Ellen nodded and tears brimmed again.

"Your Mama. She knew," Mrs. Geber said with a sigh. "She was just waiting for it to come. No life for some time now, she told me. We keep thinking, 'It will come. It will come.' But then she started with feet and hands swollen." Mrs. Geber shook her head, "That's bad sign."

Papa came in. "You want to go home now?"

Mrs. Geber nodded. "Nothing more to do. Praying I can do at home." She went to Mama's room and came back

84

with a bundle tied tight in an old cotton blanket. "I wash these," she whispered. "She should not see so much so young."

Ellen pretended not to hear her.

Papa tried to thank her but she dismissed him with an impatient gesture. "She'd do it for me."

When the door closed behind them, Ellen tiptoed to Mama's open door. Mama was sleeping with her mouth partly open and her face was even whiter than this morning—if that were possible. Ellen felt her legs weaken. Her teeth began to chatter like she was standing out in a blizzard. She wanted to run into the pantry, close the door and cry and cry. The little ones! Little footsteps upstairs. Legs shaking, she ran up to get them.

No sooner were the little ones downstairs when the school boys charged in. Ellen grabbed all three in one swoop and hissed," You boys be *quiet*! Mama's awful sick. The doctor was here."

They froze. Wide-eyed.

"We never had a doctor before," Len whispered.

"Yeah! Wait till I tell the kids at school," George said and hung his head, immediately ashamed.

"Boys! I want those woodboxes kept full and the slop pail empty. You hear? I won't yell—I'll just tell Papa."

Three heads nodded as she released them as Minnie came in.

"Hey, Minnie! The doctor was here and . . ." Eddie gushed.

"An' Ma's awful sick," Len added.

"Never mind! I'll tell her. Out! Out!"

She put her arm around confused little Minnie and explained that Mama was sick, that the doctor had come to take care of her, and now she had to stay in bed and get well, and they had a lot of work to do—but not one word about the baby.

"Who's going to cook and bake bread and take care of the little ones and wash and clean and . . ."

"Whoa now! Take it easy! Don't worry! Mrs. Geber will help some and I'll stay home from school—and you can help me."

"I can set table and make beds and dry dishes."

"I know you can. And playing with the little ones helps a lot too. Now go change your dress and put on an apron." Oh, my goodness, Ellen thought, I'm sounding like Mama already!

Papa came in and found Ellen staring at one loaf of bread. "I don't know what to have for supper and this is all the bread there is and we'll need it for lunches tomorrow."

"What would your Ma do?"

"Sometimes she makes pancakes when we run short of bread."

"Good idea. Know how?"

"I think so."

"Better get at it. Feed the little ones first. You can't fry 'em fast enough to keep up with all of us."

Ellen set the two big frying pans on the hottest stove lids and mixed a big bowl of batter.

She began frying and Minnie started setting the table while the little ones played contentedly in a corner and the boys were still outside.

Papa washed his hands, went to Mama's room and came out with the cradle and quickly carried it upstairs. No one saw him but Ellen. "If I start crying I'll get everyone upset," she thought and bit her lip. Maybe it wouldn't hurt so much now if she hadn't been angry whenever she'd looked at it waiting there.

Amazingly quiet, the boys brought in wood and water.

Papa came downstairs and said, "Make some tea with lots of sugar and milk in it." He stood staring out of the window rubbing his bristly jawline with his dry, rough hand. It made a sound Ellen could hear even above the sizzling pancakes.

He took the tea to Mama but in a few minutes he brought back the full cup. "Maybe later," he said. "Fix me a plate of pancakes. I'll feed Roy."

The school boys came in, washed without scuffling and sat down and waited patiently to be served. "Good boys!" Papa said, and they looked down to hide their pleased grins.

She had to mix more batter for Al and Fred. How did Mama do it? She felt like she might fall right on her face she was so tired.

"Here, you eat now," Papa said. "I'll fry the rest." She didn't argue.

"This is the last dish towel," Minnie said when they began washing dishes.

"Oh, golly! I didn't wash today, Papa! Mama always washes on Monday," Ellen wailed.

"Fred can help you tomorrow," Papa said, putting on his coat to go out and do chores. "I don't want you to hang out clothes and get your sore throat back. What would we do if *you* got sick?"

Had she ever felt so important? It felt good.

After the children were in bed she still had to set the yeast for bread tomorrow and get quilts down from upstairs to make Papa's bed on the couch the way he'd asked her to. Where she would find enough energy to get through that next half hour she simply didn't know.

Papa sat down in the front room near the heater stove and smoked his pipe and rocked. He looked slightly relieved since Mama had sipped a little tea after supper.

Ellen finished making his bed and looked in at Mama. "Papa? Can I say good night to her?"

He nodded.

A strange unpleasant odor hung in the little room. Mingled with it was the familiar sweet smell of frying pancakes. If it were only warm enough to open a window. It obviously wasn't bothering Mama. She was lying the same as Ellen had seen her several hours before. Ellen bent and kissed her dry hot forehead.

"Good night, Mama," she whispered, choking back a sob.

Mama's dry lips moved. The words came slowly. "Sleep good, Ellie girl."

Ellen walked quickly past Papa into the pantry, pulled the door shut behind her and sobbed over the flour barrel.

Like a huge black hawk swooping low over a defenseless chick, guilt hovered over her. She cowered over the barrel unable to find refuge.

Mama! Mama! You still think of others as sick as you are. It's all my fault . . . all my fault. If I hadn't been so selfish. . . .

She cried herself empty and tiptoed upstairs, undressed in the dark and fell into bed, pleading, "Please, God! Please, God!"

Attempting to Cope

As always Ellen's first thought Tuesday morning was, "What day is this?" The day established, a welter of prospects for the day tumbled into her mind like windfall apples. She sorted them, rejected some, picked others for closer inspection and chose a few worth keeping. On those she hinged the day.

Usually morning thoughts evoked only shallow emotions. Not today. *Mama's sick. Terribly sick!* The thought crashed in on her like the roof of a makeshift playhouse. *The baby's dead.* Her pulse raced. *It's all my fault!* A chill set her trembling, and she ducked her head under the covers to escape the hawk of guilt still swooping low.

"Ellie! Time to get up," Papa called, attempting to keep his voice low. The hawk vanished.

Her head popped out. "I'm coming," she called. Back under she went. Have to think of something—just *one* thing to look forward to today.

She was nearly dressed when she finally thought of something. Washing clothes alone for the first time was something special. Fred would help but she'd be in charge. Clean clothes are important. Nice fresh nighties for Mama, clean towels. . . .

Papa was putting wood in the cookstove when she came down.

"How's Mama?"

He shook his head. "Not good. I'll get the boys started with chores and come back in. Try to get her to drink something." He hardly looked like Papa with two days' growth of whiskers, hair tousled and his eyes puffy.

Ellen put water on for tea, started coffee and got out the cup and saucer with the roses. As she carried the tea, she steadied the cup with her left hand when it danced on the saucer. "Stop shaking!" she commanded herself.

Rosy spots burned high on Mama's cheeks, but still she lay with her eyes shut, breathing rapidly.

"Mama?" Ellen whispered. No response.

"Mama?" Ellen said a little louder, gently soothing her forehead.

Mama's eyes opened and she tried to wet her lips.

"Tea?" Ellen carefully lowered a spoonful. Mama took it. She took another, and another, and another and she was asleep again.

Ellen left the cup, ran to the kitchen, put water on for corn mush, sliced the remaining bread as thin as possible and ran back to give Mama more tea. Four more sips. Ellen dressed little Roy, combed Minnie's hair, buttoned Gertie's dress and hurried back to Mama.

Mama refused the tea. "Bring me the baby," she whispered.

Ellen backed into the front room, face contorted, hand over her mouth just as Papa came in. "She—she wants the *baby!*"

Papa was at her side, gripping her shoulders. "She doesn't remember. Get hold of yourself now—don't upset the little ones!"

Back in the kitchen she could still feel Papa's fingers gripping her shoulders, demanding control.

"Start eating," Papa said and went to Mama's room. A moment later he came back and whispered to Al, "Go get Mrs. Geber as soon as you're done eating."

Al left his corn mush, gulped his milk and left.

Throat aching, stomach queasy, Ellen managed to ease the family through breakfast and gave the school children a reassuring smile and a cheerful good-bye.

"Where do I start?" she mumbled. "Better mix the bread first and make buns for dinner. Bread won't be done." A scream. She ran and picked up little Roy with flour-covered hands. A blue bump was rising on Roy's forehead.

"John pushed him!" Gertie yelled.

"Did not!"

"You did too push him!"

Papa came in. "Here! Here!" A frown at John, a pat for Roy. Peace restored.

Stickly mess, bread. There now, one, two, three, turn. One, two, three, turn. Please, God, help Mama. Please, God, help Mama!

If only Mrs. Geber would come. Got to think about dinner. Boil potatoes in the peelings for frying. . . . Dog barking. Thank goodness. Mrs. Geber's here.

"Will you have some coffee?"

"Later, my girl. Later." Mrs. Geber set a jar on the table. "Beef broth," she said and hurried to Mama.

It was nearly eleven when Mrs. Geber poured herself a cup of coffee and sat down, watching Ellen scrub clothes on the washboard.

"You eat anything this morning?"

Ellen straightened and rubbed her back. "I guess not."

91

"Dry your hands. Sit down. Want eggs scrambled or plain?"

"Oh, Mrs. Geber, I'll fix myself something."

"You sit. White as the sheets, you are. Even horses eat!"

"I—I forgot. Scrambled, please." Tears welled up as soon as she relaxed. "It's good to be busy when things are bad, ain't it?"

"Busy, ya. A blessing it is we can't think of two things at once. To think about work—it helps, but you must whenever you can rest and when you rest—you eat!"

If someone else talked all mixed up like that it might irk me, Ellen thought, but Mrs. Geber . . . it didn't matter.

At dinner time Fred washed dishes and Ellen dried. "How does Mama do it, Fred? She never has wash water sitting here at noon and she does it all alone. I still have overalls to wash."

Fred shrugged. "I know one thing. She's going to need help when she gets better. That's for sure."

"I heard Papa and Mrs. Geber talking about having the doctor come back tomorrow, but they decided he can't do anything anyway."

"I never prayed so much in my life."

"Me, too."

How little she really knew Fred. She'd never thought of Fred feeling things deeply—or praying. She felt very close to him now and it comforted her.

At Mrs. Geber's insistence, Papa took Gertie and Roy upstairs for a nap and lay down with them. John, fast outgrowing naps, went outside with Al.

From the front room rocker where she could see Mama, Mrs. Geber kept vigil. She had brought her knitting but occasionally her head fell back, her eyes closed and the knitting lay idle.

Mama slept on and on—the sleep of the very ill. Her

breathing was still shallow, the pulse in her temple beat like the heart of a little bird, and her face, haggard now instead of bloated, often contorted as if in pain. If Mama had asked for the baby again Ellen didn't know it, because Papa and Mrs. Geber had erected an invisible barrier beyond which the family ventured at the risk of a withering frown from one or both of them. Even little Roy regarded Mama with awe and went no closer than the front room door.

Papa came down bleary eyed before the little ones woke up, stropped his razor and mixed shaving soap. Ellen watched him out of the corner of her eye, seeking reassurance. She found none. Instead of deft strokes with his straight-edged razor, accompanied by humming, he grimaced and let out his breath in little grunts as he shaved. Smooth faced again, he urged Mrs. Geber to go home and rest, put on his coat and went outside.

"I'll go see your mama," Mrs. Geber sighed, "and then I'll go home; but you send Al for me," she added quickly, "if there is any change—if she needs me. Make her drink, drink, drink."

Wednesday was a repetition of Tuesday with only slight variations. Even the school boys maintained unbelievable silence—their eyes forever questioning.

Only those searching eyes kept Ellen's face composed, her movements and her manner calm. But assurance that Mama was better she could not offer—not until there was reason for it.

Thursday morning, Mama still lay unresponsive. It took every particle of willpower Ellen possessed to begin the day's work instead of sobbing her heart out over the flour barrel.

That afternoon Aunt Clara and Uncle Walter came. No one ever visited during the week. Sundays were for visiting. Not that Ellen wasn't glad to have them come but now she *was* concerned. They wouldn't have come if Mama wasn't seriously ill.

It was almost like having Mama around to have Aunt Clara in the house. Mrs. Geber, Aunt Clara's mother, was nice, but Ellen couldn't talk to her like she could to Aunt Clara. Mama was always so glad to see her, but today she was unaware of anyone around her.

Uncle Walter took Mrs. Geber home; Papa went upstairs to nap, and Aunt Clara sat with Mama, cooling her face with a damp cloth and trying to get her to take sips of broth or tea.

Ellen sorted and folded clothes, thinking of how many hours Clara had spent with Mama in the little log house those long winter weeks when Papa worked in the lumber camp and came home only weekends. Before Clara married Mama's brother, Walter, she often stayed the night with Mama and helped her with her babies.

Aunt Clara came and sat down by the table where Ellen was working.

"She doesn't seem to even know I'm there. I'll visit with you a little while. How are you doing, Ellen?"

"Oh, all right, I guess, but I never get done with the work."

"Don't let that worry you. I never do, either."

"Aunt Clara? How is Mama?" She looked straight at Aunt Clara's eyes, knowing what she told her would be the truth.

"Nobody knows for sure—not even a doctor could tell how sick she is, but by the way she breathes and the fever she has we know she is a very sick woman. Ma thinks there will be a change in another day."

A tear dripped on the gray flannel shirt Ellen was folding and spread like ink on a blotter.

Clara shut the door to the front room and put her arms around Ellen. "Now you go ahead and cry if you want to.

You just have to let it out, girl."

Two days' accumulation of sobs poured out while Clara patted Ellen's back and offered her a hankie when she quieted down.

"I'm no doctor, but I can tell you I feel that she's going to be all right. I can't explain it. I just *feel* it."

"Thanks. That helps."

Clara wiped her own eyes and said, "If only little Anne was well she could help and you could go back to school. Don't know what to do with that girl. She's had such a bad cough all winter. I'm afraid to let her come. You folks don't need any more sickness."

"Thank You for letting Aunt Clara come today, dear Lord," Ellen prayed that night. Over and over she reassured herself with Aunt Clara's words—"I feel she's going to be all right." She just *had* to be right.

Friday dawned dishrag gray. Ellen woke still weary. Little by little she felt her energy wearing away each day—like a bar of soap one didn't realize was dissolving until one day it broke. "But I can't break," she told herself. "I have to keep going."

At noon Papa told them to begin eating without him, while he tried to get Mama to take some tea. Al dished up a heap of fried potatoes, slapped two fried eggs on top of it and chopped it up so the soft yolks coated the potatoes, grumbling into his shirt front.

"What'd you say?" Ellen asked.

"He says he wants to know when we're getting something besides potatoes and eggs around here," Fred reported, preferring a squabble to monotony.

Faced with the choice of a campaign of self-defense or a bid of sympathy, Ellen chose the latter, pushing back her chair slowly enough for Al to see her eyes filling but quickly enough to be dramatic, and ducked into the pantry. She cried a little while but she knew Al would never come and get her, so she took her place again with loud sniffs.

Gertie laid her head possessively on Ellen's arm and glared at Al, and Al said brightly, "Know what I'm going to do when I earn some money? I'm going to get a good camera and all the stuff and I'm going to have my own darkroom and develop and print my own pictures. How'd you like your picture taken, Ellie?"

"Oh, listen to that, Fred! He's not just going to take pictures—he's going to even print them!" She rolled her eyes at his preposterous notion and then winked back at Fred, who had made sure Al had seen him wink at Ellen.

"Now, Ellie. Don't make fun of Al," he said in mock seriousness. "Just wait 'til you see those pictures!"

"You think I can't! You think I can't! I'll show you!" Al pushed his chair back with such a loud scrape Papa came out of the bedroom with his eyes blazing.

"What in thunder's wrong with you? Noise like that makes her quiver all over. She's whimpering in there like a beaten pup."

Al mumbled an apology and slunk outside.

Fred and Ellen began washing dishes as quietly as possible.

"I feel awful," Ellen said with a sniff. "I didn't mean to disturb Mama."

"You didn't. It was my fault for makin' Al mad."

Mama says there's always something to be thankful for in every bad situation, Ellen thought. I'd never have known Fred like this if Mama hadn't got sick.

That night, almost too tired to blow out the lamp, Ellen crawled into bed with a groan. The lengthy prayer she had intended to offer became: "Please, God! Please, God!" and she slept.

There was something different about Mama when Ellen peeked in at her Saturday morning. She was resting on her side with one hand under her cheek and her mouth wasn't open.

There was something different about Papa, too. There was a light in his eyes though he still didn't smile.

A little later, Papa brought Mama's empty tea cup while Minnie and Ellen were cooking breakfast and said, "She wants to know why we don't give her something to eat!" He was *smiling!*

The dog announced Mrs. Geber's arrival. She bustled in to see Mama, and came out with her hands clasped in front of her and her face radiant. "Praise *Gott*. She is better!"

Papa nodded and smiled. "During the night she reached for the water glass. Almost spilled it, she's so shaky, but she tried!" He cleared his throat and reached for his coat, blinking hard.

When they were alone Ellen grabbed Minnie and whirled her around the room, laughing and crying at the same time. "We'd better not tell the boys yet or they'll never shut up!" Ellen said when they sat down to catch their breaths.

Minnie's smile faded. "Ellie? Did you think she was gonna die?"

"Of course not!" Ellen fibbed.

"Well, I did," Minnie said, tears threatening to spill over.

Ellen hugged her. "Oh, honey, she's going to be *all right!*"

"Will she get up today?"

"Oh, no. Not for several days probably. She's awful weak, you know. Let's work real hard so the house looks nice when she gets up." Ellen jumped to her feet, thankful Minnie hadn't asked what was wrong with Mama. Oh, to be like Minnie—innocent and guilt free!

Even Minnie's chatter couldn't annoy her as she flew from task to task with visions of Mama well again. She could see Mama, heat flushed but smiling over a fragrant pot of soup—Mama pinning the brooch on her Sunday dress, humming "Blessed Assurance, Jesus Is Mine"— Mama exchanging a smile with Papa over the little ones' heads—Mama, her head to one side, admiring freshly washed curtains. "I'll never get angry and glare at her again," Ellen told the geranium in the south window.

Before Mrs. Geber went home, she helped Mama sit up and put her feet on the floor for just a minute. "Have to get the blood moving," Mrs. Geber explained. "Ellen, when Clara comes tomorrow tell her to help your ma sit up again. I won't come tomorrow long as Clara'll be here."

After supper Papa pushed back his chair—quietly— and said, "I want you to know your ma is better." He shook his finger at the boys who were ready to let out a whoop. "Ah, ah! None of that. We'll have it quiet around here awhile." He pointed to little Roy. "That goes for you too, young man." Little Roy grinned his four-teeth grin and banged a spoon on the table before Ellen could grab his chubby fist. Gertie and John giggled themselves under the table, and everyone else laughed disproportionately hard until Papa frowned and shook his head and the laughter instantly subsided.

Minnie tugged at his arm. "Don't it feel good to laugh, Papa? I was afraid I forgot how."

He reached out and encircled her in an affectionate gesture he reserved for the very young, and Minnie rested her head on his shoulder in sheer bliss.

Aunt Clara and Uncle Walter came Sunday afternoon. "I can't wait to see for myself," Aunt Clara said, pulling off her coat and hurrying to Mama's room. "Your papa says she's better."

She was back in a short while, blowing her nose. "She's Emma again. She really is!" She hugged Ellen and held her at arms' length. "You look so tired. You go rest awhile. I brought stew for supper."

Snuggled deep under the quilts, Ellen smiled, sighed and slept. At first when she woke up she thought it was morning, but it was afternoon light, not morning light in her room. What was that? Her heart thumped. Mama was crying. Like snow birds scatter when the door slams, her happiness took wing and in its place the hawk hung low. She hid under the covers. "How could I forget about the baby and that Mama would be sad when she realized what had happened? All I thought about was myself—how glad I'd be to get back to school!" She heard Aunt Clara's voice, but she couldn't understand what she said, and then she heard Mama say, "It's like a bad dream, Clara," and she cried some more.

Ellen put her fingers in her ears so she couldn't hear Mama cry. If it were Bible times, she thought, I could wear sackcloth and ashes to show how sorry I am. She could see herself sitting behind the heater stove in a gray heap. "What on earth are you doing?" Papa would say, and she'd groan and beat her chest and show him how penitent she was. Crazy thoughts! What *could* she do? "If I work real hard—don't think about myself at all . . ."

The roar of the coffee grinder snapped her back to reality and she scrambled out of bed and ran downstairs.

Aunt Clara was filling the coffee pot. "Have a good rest?"

Ellen nodded and escaped to the pantry. Aunt Clara followed her. "You heard your mama crying."

Ellen nodded—averting her eyes. If Aunt Clara only knew . . .

"Now, now, don't feel so bad. She was too sick to remember what happened and now she had to cry it out."

She patted Ellen's shoulder. "Your mama's proud of how well you've taken over the work. We all are."

Papa and Uncle Walter came in and Aunt Clara rushed out. Ellen began slicing bread. She gleaned no happiness from the praise. Maybe—if she explained very carefully just how she had felt about the baby coming, Aunt Clara would understand. It would be so good to tell someone all about it. But what if she didn't understand? She tried to imagine Aunt Clara frowning, condemning, scolding instead of smiling so affectionately. She shivered. Anyway . . . there was no time to tell her now. Everyone was coming in for supper. Next week she'd tell her.

Before they left, Ellen remembered to tell Aunt Clara to help Mama sit up. She watched from the front room while Mama, hair wild about her face, sat swaying in Aunt Clara's arms. It would be a long while before Mama was well and bustling around the house again.

"It's only a week. It takes awhile," Mrs. Geber reminded Papa Monday morning when he thought Mama should be able to sit up longer.

"Only a week," Ellen grumbled to herself, plunging a stack of breakfast plates into the dishwater. "Must have washed a million already."

Yesterday's vows of penitence now dim, she fumbled her groggy way through the morning work.

Later she was grateful for a break from the washboard when Mrs. Geber called her. Mama was sitting vacant-eyed on a chair in her room while Mrs. Geber held her steady. "You want to brush your mama's hair?"

Ever so carefully Ellen brushed out snarls, supporting Mama's head with her left hand when it drooped. She lifted Mama's feet into bed when Mrs. Geber finished making it.

Mama sighed from her smooth pillow and thanked them

with a wan smile.

All the while Mrs. Geber got ready to go home, she told Ellen what a good nurse she would make and how lucky Mama was to have her.

When the door closed behind her, Ellen scrubbed a woolen sock like she would scrub her very soul if it were possible. She pushed the compliment out of her mind but she began visualizing herself in a full-skirted, tight-waisted nurse's uniform with a stiff cap perched high on her dark hair. She could hear her skirts rustle as she strode efficiently down a long corridor. There were long corridors in hospitals. She knew that because Miss McKinley had told her all about hospitals with beds high and smooth as loaves of rising bread and not a speck of dust anywhere —and doctors giving orders to nurses and nuns.

Did every hospital have nuns? Have to ask Miss McKinley. The nuns she had seen on the street in Tomahawk with yards and yards of black clothing floating as they walked—did they work in all that?

"Ouch!" she yelled when Fred jabbed her in the ribs with his elbow. "What'd you do that for?"

"For crying out loud, I asked you three times what we're having for dinner?"

"Oh my gosh! It's half past eleven. I never even thought about dinner." A shock flashed through her, but it seeped away when she remembered there was still some of Aunt Clara's stew and some fat molasses cookies, too. Bless Aunt Clara!

After dinner Fred took John outside, the little ones slept, and Ellen settled down for a whole afternoon of daydreaming. She could see doctors with soft white hands like Dr. Pearson's. She accepted their praise for her efficient work with humility and poise. She did dishes and dreamed, churned butter and dreamed some more, and when Mama needed care she wore her imaginary uniform, wishing she had nothing to do but care for Mama.

The school children burst in and put an abrupt end to her pleasant afternoon. At the same time, Fred dumped armloads of half-dry clothes on the table she had forgotten to wipe off after dinner. She flung the clothes over the line in back of the stove and finished the butter she had left standing when she went to take care of Mama. She started peeling potatoes and forgot them when little Roy woke up—then let the cookstove fire go out and yelled at Minnie for talking so much. Minnie ran howling upstairs, and Papa and the boys came in for supper and it was hardly started. If those boys made one smart remark. . . . They disappointed her by being unusually patient and deprived her of an excuse to vent her frustration.

Much later, after an unbelievably difficult supper hour, she gave the flour barrel several good kicks and informed it that she was never never never going to get married and have a bunch of kids!

It took Ellen almost no time to find something to look forward to Tuesday morning. She'd invent patients with all sorts of illnesses and injuries. Why, she hadn't even had a good start yesterday.

When Mrs. Geber called her to brush Mama's hair, Mama became a real live patient. She brought a fresh glass of water and stood at attention while Mrs. Geber gave her orders for the afternoon. Later, as she put prunes to soak, she wished she had a whole row of patients like Mama to care for.

At noon she pulled the shade on her dream scenes and hardly got any worthwhile dreaming done at all that afternoon, because Gertie and John didn't go to sleep and made so much commotion she had to invent something to keep them quiet. Turned-over chairs and an old quilt made a good playhouse—until little Roy woke up and insisted on pulling it down. "Am I glad to see you!" she told Minnie when she got home from school. "Maybe you can keep these kids quiet."

Wednesday Mama held her head quite steady when Ellen brushed her hair and insisted she could feed herself. "Mmm, that looks good!" she said when Ellen brought her a bowl of pitted prunes with heavy cream. "Why don't you fix yourself some and join me?

"Feels like I just got back from a long trip," Mama said.

"You were real sick, Mama."

She sighed. "I'm afraid it will take me a little while to get strong again. Sure hate having you miss so much school."

"Don't worry. I'll make it up."

"How're you doing with the work?"

"Pretty good. Never get done, though."

"Women never do, I guess. Helps to finish one job at a time, though. Some women piddle around here, piddle around there—never finish anything. You know what I mean."

I know what she means, all right, Ellen thought as she carried their bowls to the kitchen. She's been listening and knows what a mess I get myself into. If she was up she'd be scolding like everything, but now she lies there and thinks about how she can get me to see my mistakes.

Thursday when Mrs. Geber was getting ready to leave, she said, "Your mama says I shouldn't come tomorrow—that you can manage. What do you think?"

"Oh, I can do it. I'm sure I can—but I don't know how we could have gotten along without you all these days."

"*Ach!* That's nothing. You remember—anytime you think you need me, send one of the boys. I come!" Ellen helped her into her threadbare coat, wishing she dared to hug her.

It was a free feeling Friday morning to know she was completely in charge. She decided she would do things just like Mama would do them today.

To the delight of the little ones, Mama sat in the rocker for awhile before dinner. Roy sat on her lap and grinned and snuggled against her, while Gertie stroked her flannel sleeve. "Now you ain't sick anymore, huh?"

Mama kissed her forehead. "No, *Liebchen*. Just lazy." She winked at John who stood way across the room like he was afraid to go near her. He let out a whoop, ran in crazy circles and rolled a lopsided somersault.

"You almost did it! Try again. There. That's better!"

Gertie ran to try too, and got kicked in the head. She cried as long as she could against Mama's shoulder. Mama turned tired eyes toward Ellen, and Ellen lured them away with milk and cookies while she helped Mama back to bed.

She was close to tears as she went back to putting bread dough in pans. At this rate she'd never get back to school, Mama was *so* weak.

She was still feeling sorry for herself an hour later when she put wood in the stove. Suddenly she saw those flannel pieces she had poked so angrily into the coals weeks ago, and all the ugly thoughts she had had those days poured into her mind like sand through a hole. How could she keep forgetting how awful she had been?

At noon Papa noticed her dejection and asked her if she was all right. She told him she was fine and gave him a strained smile. While she washed dishes she tried to figure out how she should act. Sad? Humble? Confident? Serene? Capable? Dependable? It must be so wonderful to be grown-up and always know just how to act. She'd know how to act as a nurse. Here was refuge for the afternoon. She was still "nursing" when the school children came home.

She woke startled and shivering during the night. She

had dreamed her bed was right out in the open snow-blown field. She scooted deeper under the covers, drew her feet up and listened to the wind that shook the house with such force she half expected the windows to give way.

She slept again and woke a long while later to white light cast by abundant new snow. The wind, less eerie in the light, still tested its strength against the staunch house, eased its attack as if resting, then struck again with new indignation, slinging snow against the window.

Saturday. No school. What could she possibly find to look forward to with two whole days of being cooped up with all the other people. She groaned. Her stomach growled. Breakfast. Pancakes! That was it! Crisp edged—melted butter sliding off—she'd hurry and fry hers first and then, comfortably full, she'd fry and fry for all the others.

Papa and the big boys were already outside when she came down. She mixed the batter in the pantry so no one would hear her and set the big black pans on to heat ever so quietly. She poured pools of batter into the sizzling grease.

Thumps overhead! More thumps! She dashed for butter, syrup, a plate and a fork.

Hard bare feet thundering down the stairs!

She flipped the pancakes—brown-edged to perfection, mouth watering as she inhaled their aroma. The hall door flew open so hard it bounced against the wall and George, Len and Ed charged to the stove.

"We smelled 'em!" Eddie yelled, grinning broadly. "You make good pancakes, Ellie!"

"That's my pan full. That's my pan full!" George yelled in her ear.

She wanted to hit him.

Len stood beside her. "You was all set to eat 'em, huh?" he said, pointing to her plate and fork.

She nodded. "I was." He backed away. Head down.

"Oh, go get your plates. I can't do everything."

She nipped a brown edge and nibbled it while she poured more batter into the pans. "Pour your own milk, too. You're not babies!"

They were back clamoring for more before she had even turned them. She swiped half of one of Ed's, allayed his protest with a wink and sprinkled sugar on it, rolled it up and ate it in three bites.

She never did sit down and eat. Over an hour later, legs weary, stomach full from eating quick snatches, yet unsatisfied because she had never sat down to relish them, she went to get Mama's dishes.

Mama talked about the storm, but her words skimmed the surface of Ellen's mind. She was aware only of the sweet odor of frying pancakes in the room and the emotions that odor evoked. She hurried to the pantry and clung to the flour barrel, suddenly weak. It was as though miraculously intervening time had vanished, leaving the image of Papa carrying the bright new wooden box as vividly as the day she had seen it. Where was it now? Surely Papa hadn't buried it that day. He had come back in the house in a short while. Maybe when she saw that little grave—could cry over it—put flowers on it—maybe then she'd feel better.

She tried not to think of it. Right now that baby should be snuggled warm and soft against Mama's breast—and it would be if it weren't for her! Guilt descended. Heavy. Black. Smothering. She cowered beneath it and tried to pray. How could God hear her? These past days in her long-corridored dream world she hadn't even thought about God. Could He possibly forgive her and hear her prayers now when she needed Him again?

"I'll die. I simply won't breathe and I'll . . ."

The door slammed. "Ellie!" It was Al's voice, loud and demanding.

She flew out, sustained the shock of his blood dripping into the wash basin from the gash in his left hand, and ran for clean rags.

She soaped his grimy hand and poured warm water over it, steeling herself when he winced. "How'd it happen?"

"Splittin' wood. Hurry up! Wrap it tight!"

Hands steady, she bound it in a snug, neat bandage.

"Nice job, Ellie. Thanks," Al said and went back out, leaving her to cope with the day's work.

No sense going back to the pantry. She filled the dishpan. She didn't really want to die—not right now.

She was about to blow out the kitchen lamp at bedtime when Papa laid a weighty hand on her shoulder and said, "Your ma and me were saying a little while ago you sure had patience today with all the noise and work and mess and all. You did real well."

Another time his precious words would have borne her to bed on a cloud of elation. Not tonight. She forbade herself to take any pleasure in them. If Papa knew what she was really like inside he'd hate her as much as she hated herself—maybe more.

Keeping the Children Occupied

"It's Sunday," Ellen groaned when she woke. "Everyone will be in the house all day again." The boys would track in slush, leave the door open to icy blasts, or worse yet, slam it so hard Mama would tremble, clutch the quilts and blink back tears. Knowing that noise bothered Mama intensified every bump and thump until Ellen wanted to haul off and swat whoever caused it.

She dozed and woke again and there it was, like a geranium bud that opens during the night, something to look forward to. Something to brighten everyone's day. Taffy! She'd make taffy and they'd sit around the table and pull it. Mmm, she could taste it already. Lately she'd been so candy hungry she often ate a spoonful of sugar in spite of Mama's warning that sugar caused worms.

The anticipation of the happy faces when she announced a surprise and the thought of the taste of the taffy eased her through the morning's clamor and drudgery.

Mama approved of the taffy-pull idea, but warned Ellen it would make extra work for her. After dinner when she told them there would be a surprise as soon as dishes were done, even the school boys pitched in and helped. As soon as she poured the dishwater in the slop pail they demanded, "Tell us now! What's the surprise?"

"We're going to make taffy. Remember? We pull it 'til it gets hard and cut it in pieces. It has to cook and cool and then you'll all get some to pull."

Never had a kettle boiled so slowly. She shook down the ashes and wooed the fire with choice dry sticks and waited and waited. Minnie crowded close and peered into the kettle, and Gertie stood on the oven door and yelled, "Let me see! Let me see!" The boys clamored, "What's takin' so long? How long d'we have ta wait?"

Papa ordered them away from the stove and Ellen sighed. Next time she'd have sense enough to tell them *after* it was cooked and cooled.

She herded them to the wash basin while it cooled. "Everyone scrub your hands and you'll each get some."

"Oh, sure!" grumbled Al, waving his bandaged hand.

After a scuffle at the washstand they sat elbow-jabbing each other long before it was cool enough to handle.

"Butter your hands! Here it comes!"

The room quieted as their jaws became immobilized and Ellen exchanged smiles with Papa. Most gobs of taffy were rapidly shrinking. Fred and Ellen held their large hot masses gingerly and compared the color now and then.

"Mine's lighter than yours!"

"Ain't either."

" 'Tis too!"

The smaller portions hardened, were twisted into ropes, laid on the breadboard and chopped into inch-long pieces which promptly vanished.

Ellen's hefty rope was ready to twist, all golden and

satiny, when she looked over at Gertie.

"Oh, Gertie honey! Look at you!" Her dress front, face, hands and even her hair were flypaper consistency, and her mouth so full that slurpy drools escaped and rolled down her chin.

The boys hooted, pointed their fingers and everyone laughed.

She began to cry, further diluting the mess.

At that moment Papa escorted Mama from her room and helped her to a chair, standing with his arm around her while she rocked with laughter.

Papa caught Gertie an instant before she hurled her sticky self into Mama's lap, and Ellen led her to the wash basin.

Mama dried her eyes, accepted the several pieces of taffy proffered and smiled up at Papa. "I needed a good laugh. Haven't felt this good for a long time."

Later when Ellen put her hands in hot dishwater she winced. Blisters! No one else had any. "They were too busy eating to get blisters from pulling," Papa teased.

Monday morning the sting of strong soap in her blisters brought tears to her eyes. Mama saw her plunge them into the rinse-water.

"Oh, dear! Those blisters! Let me see," Mama said, sitting down shakily in the kitchen rocker.

Ellen turned her palms up, choking back tears. "What'll I do?"

"If only I could get my strength back . . . tell you what. Sort out just what we really need today and wash again later this week when your hands are better. Fred will have to scrub clothes today—you do the rinsing and wringing."

Mama leaned back exhausted, but out of the corner of her eyes Ellen caught Mama's smile of satisfaction. Mama felt useful again.

Fred scrubbed clothes uncomplainingly, but teased Ellen that the next time he'd see that he got blisters so he could get out of work.

Ellen splashed rinse water in his face, but he ignored it and let it run down into his grin.

Mama watched, amused. She burst out laughing. "I can still see Gertie!"

"Me, too." Ellen chuckled. "And those boys trying to look so innocent with their mouths so full." She cranked the clothes through the wringer and watched them pile up in folds like ribbon candy until they toppled into the water.

"It felt so good to laugh," Mama said. "It would have been an awful afternoon with everyone cooped up if you hadn't made that taffy. See how people can make their own fun if they really want to!"

After dinner she thought about what Mama had said. She put the little ones to bed, came back in the kitchen and stood queen-like, surveying the room with a heady sense of power. "Right here in this room I can make people happy. Maybe not all the time, but I can do it!" She leaned on the window ledge and gazed over the blue-shadowed snow. The thought came to her as vividly as if it were written letter by letter in that snow. *This is how Mama keeps going!* This room and everything in it— Mama must see it all differently. To me that stove is an insatiable old monster, demanding endless feedings of sharp-edged slivery sticks of wood and sulking at the most inopportune times. I could kick it a good one sometimes. But Mama polishes it lovingly, grateful for its grudging heat, and she remarks how cozy it sounds when it crackles. She tolerates its petulant moods as patiently as she does the cries of a hungry baby.

And potatoes! "I'm so sick of potatoes!" Ellen told the dinner dishes still waiting to be washed. She could see them firm and gritty with soil in the fall, their firmness ebbing away in winter, and in spring when one dragged them out of the bin by their long, pale sprouts, they'd be flaccid and wrinkled as aged faces. And walnut-sized summer potatoes—that made a scrunching sound and spat juice when scraped with Mama's sharp little knife that disintegrated a bit with each sharpening, until Papa predicted that one day that knife would wear away completely leaving Mama holding only the handle. And boiled potatoes with sticky old peelings that glued themselves to knife and fingers! But Mama toiled over them hardly aware of what she was doing, but her face lit up when Papa and the big boys heaped crispy fried ones on their plates or dug into a mound of butter-covered mashed potatoes and gravy with a "Mmmmm!"

Even the grease-rimmed old dishpan didn't seem to bother Mama. She often finished the last pots and pans, emptied it, wiped it dry and hung it up with an air of having accomplished a splendid feat.

Ellen shook her head. It must be so nice to be grown up and not have all these things bother you—see the purpose behind them all and not hate the work involved. She started guiltily when the clock struck one o'clock and tackled the dishes with new zeal.

Thank goodness she had finished the dishes before Mama came out and sat, with a sigh, in the kitchen rocker. "Get so tired of lying there. It's nice to sit up when it's quiet."

"Feeling better?"

She sighed. "If I wasn't so bloomin' weak . . . you should be back in school."

"I'll catch up—and besides, book learning isn't everything!"

Mama looked like she was trying not to smile. "Want to

get my knitting for me?" she said after a moment. "Maybe I can wear off some of this fidgety feeling."

"I've been thinking a lot today. A woman's powerful, ain't she?"

"Powerful?"

"Well, she can make people happy—like I did with the taffy."

Mama laughed. "Yes. I guess you could call making people happy a kind of 'power.' You've learned something important. People have to have fun. That's hard for me to remember. I think too much about getting the work done and I forget. Your papa now, he has sense enough to do something for fun. Me . . . I really don't know how to have fun."

"Oh, but you do, Mama—in your own way. You enjoy lots of things like walking in the woods down by the river, and laughing at the little ones, and admiring a pretty quilt block or the frost flowers on the windows or the little wren that nests in the hollow clothes pole every year—all sorts of things. And you've taught me to enjoy them, too."

"Ya, ya, but all too seldom." She sat with her eyes closed—the knitting lying idle in her lap. "God knows what He's doing when He puts us flat on our backs at times. We sure get a chance to look at what we've been doing and maybe even try to change. So much of our happiness is our own doing." She opened her eyes and picked up her knitting. "I always think about what I read that Abraham Lincoln once said. Let's see if I can remember it." His lips moved soundlessly. "I have it! He said, 'People are about as happy as they make up their minds to be.' I thought about that a lot." The knitting needles clicked a little while and then she continued, "Everything has to start with a thought, you know—how you feel—what you do. That's why it's so important to have good thoughts. If we go around thinking bad things

114

and wishing for things we don't have, or digging way back remembering when someone hurt our feelings, there's no time left to think about what we could do to be happy or to make others happy. Sure is hard to do sometimes—'specially when you know you've done something wrong. Your mind wants to go over it and over it." She put her knitting down and pounded her right fist into her left palm. "Been trying so hard to get my mind on pleasant things. Tried planning the garden and flower beds for spring, planned dresses I want to sew for you girls—all sorts of things, but nothing works." She put her knitting on the table with a futile gesture, got up and staggered toward her bedroom.

Ellen sprang to help her, encircling her shoulders with strong young arms. Mama's shoulders were shaking. Mama was crying! She rolled into bed and turned toward the wall and cried softly into her pillow.

"Mama!" little Roy called and climbed out of his bed.

Ellen grabbed him and took him to the kitchen. What could Mama have done wrong? What was she crying about? The baby?

On the verge of sleep that night, Ellen tried to reconstruct Mama's words. Yes, she had definitely sounded like she felt bad about doing something wrong. What did Mama ever do wrong? Oh, sure, she got angry with Mama when she scolded and all that, but that wasn't doing anything bad or hurtful . . .

"Maybe next week I can go back to school," Ellen told herself Tuesday morning. She'd work like everything the rest of the week. Mama could be a lot stronger by then.

As soon as the children left for school, Ellen stacked the dishes and began sprinkling clothes. Mama hobbled in, clutching her wrapper.

"Girl, what's the matter with you? Look what you're

doing! Minnie's sleeve just missed that milk ring. Ain't it hard enough to get clothes washed and dried without having to do it all over again? No reason why you shouldn't do those dishes first, anyway."

She stopped for breath just as Papa came in for dry mittens and continued, "Now let that sprinkling go and get those dishes washed first."

Papa frowned and went out, and Mama staggered back to bed. Ellen choked back angry words and glared at her back.

After dinner Mama came out in the kitchen and steadied herself against the reservoir. "For goodness' sakes! Don't you ever wipe this stove? There's an inch of dust back there—and look at the tea kettle. Hand me that rag!"

She wiped the cover, turned the rag over and wiped around the tea kettle, paying careful attention around the handle—all the while panting like it took all the energy she possessed. "Now throw that filthy thing away. How many times have I told you to keep a clean dishrag? Rags we've got plenty of. You want to eat from dishes washed with this filthy thing?"

Papa got up from the rocker where he had been relaxing after dinner, took Mama by the shoulders and turned her toward the bedroom. "That's where you belong," he said, "not out here bossing." He draped his long arm around her shoulders and walked her to her door.

Later when Papa had gone outside and the little ones were asleep, Mama came out and leaned against the door frame. "I want you to do something while the little ones are asleep," she whispered. "No sense giving them a chance to ask questions." She sat down heavily in the rocker. "I want you to take the box that's under my bed and put it upstairs in the cradle." She studied her clenched hands. "It's the baby clothes."

Ellen waited to be sure Mama had no more to say.

"When I'm feeling better I'll give them to someone who needs them."

"Give them away?"

Mama nodded, biting her lower lip. "Dr. Pearson says I ain't going to have any more babies. I didn't hear him say it—I was too sick, but Papa and Mrs. Geber said he told them."

"But—but can he really tell?"

"I don't know." She waved impatiently. "Now go do what I say."

Ellen eased the box out onto the braided rug beside Mama's bed, cast a furtive glance at the sleeping children, picked it up and tiptoed out.

She hesitated beside Mama. "He could be wrong, couldn't he?"

Mama looked up, eyes angry. "I told you, do what I say. Go take that . . ." Her voice broke and she gestured toward the stairway.

Ellen climbed the stairs with anger, sympathy, shock and remorse all swirling within her.

She folded back the faded blanket covering the cradle, set the box in it and lifted the lid. To the right lay several neatly folded flannel sacques trimmed with blue feather-stitching—brilliant white against the other grayed and yellowed garments and diapers. She picked one up and brushed it with her lips, then put it back quickly lest she tear stain it. She replaced the lid, pulled the blanket over it and leaned against the chimney.

"No more babies. Ever!" she whispered, but her mind didn't want to absorb those words. It was as though a door had clanged shut, closing off a dark corridor of her mind. She turned and flattened herself against the warm chimney, aware of uncomfortable pressure against her breasts. For the moment she had no desire to beat down the barrier to that blocked corridor. For the moment she felt safe and warm and loved, and time was nonexistent. She drifted through pleasant scenes—like flipping through pages of a picture book seeing water swirling between gleaming black rocks, golden cowslips, violets, maples, ice-covered—glistening in the sun. May flowers pushing plushy heads through wet leaves, and maple sap drip, drip, dripping. Red sunsets turning purple and dark sky splendorous with stars. Papa carrying a lantern and eerie shadows swinging far across the snow as he walked. Daylight. Papa walking toward the barn carrying a . . . no! No! She refused to see it! She swiveled around. Heart beating fast. What am I doing here? What time is it? Afternoon. Mama's sitting up in the rocker. Got to get busy!

She hurried down and found the rocker empty. Somewhat relieved, she went back to ironing, grasping the iron awkwardly to skirt her blisters, and sorted through her mind for pleasant thoughts—anything to avoid that intolerable corridor—sunlight and green-grass thoughts drifting lightly on her mind's surface like a cork on water to fill the afternoon. And light thoughts she found—enough to fill the afternoon until Mama sat up and amused the little ones and the school children came home.

"Got something for ya!" George yelled. "Say please!"

"Please!" she said, holding out her hand.

"Guess which hand," he said, holding something behind him.

When she pointed to the left he said she was wrong. When she pointed to the right he said it was wrong until she struggled to get it.

"Ma! He won't give it to me!"

"George! That's enough. Give it to her!"

Grudgingly he let her grab it and she fled to the front room couch and unfolded a piece of paper, thrilled to see Miss McKinley's neat handwriting.

"Dear Ellen,

I've asked the boys repeatedly how your mother is feeling and all they say is 'All right.' I do hope she is better. The boys didn't say what is wrong and Minnie didn't seem to know, either.

When do you think you will be back to school? Would you like me to send work for you? Don't worry about your school work, however. I know you will catch up in a short while.

Come back soon. I miss you.

Sincerely,

Miss McKinley"

Ellen handed Mama the note and Mama read it and handed it back with a smile. "That was real nice of her to take time to write to you." Mama closed her eyes a little while. "Ella, tell her you'll be back to school Monday. Tell her your ma is doing fine and that it was ah . . . ah . . ." She paused and looked around as though she hoped to see the answer written on the oilcloth-covered table, the braided rug under her feet, or perhaps on the oven door. Finding none, she continued. "Tell her it was female trouble. She'll understand."

Later, as she worked in the pantry, Ellen shuddered. Horrid word, "female." Animallike. She'd write and tell Miss McKinley exactly what was wrong—including who was to blame. She'd throw herself at Miss McKinley's mercy—hide nothing. Miss McKinley would understand and forgive her if she told her what it was like to be the oldest girl, how much work there was, how tired she was of working and never having time for fun. She'd tell her how she had hoped Mama would lose it when it was hardly anything at all—not when it was about to be born. She'd tell her how she never dreamed it would cause all this trouble for Mama and how terribly sorry she was. . . .

Papa and the big boys came in for supper. A dozen things to do at once. No time to think now.

She rushed through supper dishes, grunted responses to Minnie and ran upstairs as soon as she could.

Huddled over a piece of paper backed by a copy of "The Youth's Companion," she wet the tip of the pencil on her tongue and wrote:

"Dear Miss McKinley:

I was glad to get your letter. Mama says I can come back Monday. I'm so glad."

She hadn't fully realized until she wrote it that Mama had said she could go back Monday. Suddenly she wanted to dance around the room—holler out the window, "I'm going back to school! I'm going back to school!"

Enough of this! Minnie would be coming to bed before she finished if she didn't hurry.

Pencil poised, she stared at the paper. No words came. She wandered to the frost-covered window, sat down again and followed the feather stitching around the crazy-patch quilt with her pencil. She'd start way back. Tell her about how it was to have Mama moaning and groaning around the house before she had her babies—what it was like when Mama was up nights with a crying new baby and cross as the dickens during the day because she was tired. She'd *make* Miss McKinley see she hadn't meant any harm—that she didn't want the baby to die—not when it was a real live baby big enough to be born—big enough to be put in a. . . . Oh, God! I didn't want it to die! I didn't want it to die! Great shattering sobs sent her burrowing under her pillow. They washed open the door of her mind that had shut so resolutely this afternoon, exposing the terrible truth. There would be no more Verleger babies. Not ever. But then, but then Mama would never have to groan and struggle and be up nights. She'd be well and strong and singing! The anguish was gone now. Only sadness left. She cried softly until the sadness too drained away, sat up, dried her eyes and blew her nose. Now she'd write.

How silly! She'd never be able to write all that. She'd tell her all about it after school sometime. She wet the pencil again and wrote, "Mama says to tell you she had," Ellen grimaced, "some female trouble. She said you'd understand. Thank you for writing to me. Your pupil, Ellen Verleger."

Harsh Criticism

Len was sitting on the oven door lacing his boots when Ellen came downstairs Wednesday morning.

"How come you're up already?"

"Going with Pa."

"Where?"

"Rib Lake. Don't ya remember? He said last night he was hauling the last load of bark to Rib Lake today and it's my turn to go along."

"I forgot."

"You'd better get breakfast in a hurry. Pa wants to leave by seven. I gotta get the horses ready." The door slammed behind him.

Breakfast wasn't ready when Papa came in. "Oh, well, I have to shave anyway. Might's well do it first," he said.

Ellen flashed him a grateful smile as he mixed his shaving soap, humming little snatches of an unrecognizable tune. "Don't cook any meat for supper. I've got a taste for pickled herring. I'll bring a keg." He cleared a neat swath along his jawline and gestured with the sudsy razor. "Just boil some little potatoes with the peelings."

George came downstairs and Ellen sent him for a pail of water.

Len burst in, almost knocking George over. "Horses are ready, Pa."

Papa nodded and sat down to eat.

George came in slopping water at intervals all the way across the room. "It's my turn next time, huh, Pa?"

"Ja. Your turn next. Now look at that floor. Get the mop—and for gosh sakes tie those boot laces before you break your neck."

As Ellen tied sandwiches in a clean towel she wished she could thank Tom Blanton, the former school master, who had insisted that a trip to town was worth three days in school. Succeeding teachers no longer shared Tom Blanton's conviction, but the Verleger children took turns going to town regardless.

Mama got up before they left and insisted that Len wear one more sweater. He wore it in spite of his protests that he wouldn't be able to move, let alone run.

Mama, Ellen and the little ones waved from the window as they drove out of the driveway with the big, dark load of bark.

Ellen sighed. "Don't you wish you were going?"

"Well, no. Not today. I'm mighty glad to be in a nice warm house." She squeezed Ellen's arm. "You'll get to go when it's warmer. Maybe to Tomahawk—that will be even more fun. Like to see Rib Lake, but there's something special about Tomahawk and crossing the Wisconsin river. Always wish I could get out to one of those islands and just see what's out there." She shrugged. "Silly. Just more trees, no doubt, but islands seem so mysterious."

Mama went back to bed, and Ellen sat down to enjoy a

piece of bread and raspberry jam. Five more days before Monday. She'd get some extra work done so it wouldn't be so hard for Mama next week. She could polish the stove, for one thing. Even though it gave her trouble, Ellen shared Mama's pride in the stove. It seemed like such a little while since that day when she was playing down by the river, when a wagon drawn by a mule team clattered to a stop in front of the old house. She ran up the bank and saw a fat man stand up and clang two iron frying pans together. They made a ring that echoed far up and down the river, bringing Papa and the boys home on a run. Mama bustled out of the house with the younger children spilling out around her, holding their ears.

The men shouted greetings, then rolled up the canvas on the back of the covered wagon. There it stood—the nickel trim gleaming in the sun and the copper reservoir glowing next to the shining black. A thinner man sent a lid sailing onto the large flat rock that served as a doorstep. It landed with a ringing clang, and Papa picked it up shaking his head in amazement. "Well, I'll be . . . you'd think it woulda broke clean in half!"

"If you think that's strong watch this!" The fat man jumped nimbly from the oven door to the cooking surface and back down again. "You can see, Ma'am, that I weigh well over two hundred pounds. Now when did you ever put anything on your stove that weighed over two hundred pounds? And if you did—it sure wouldn't be jumpin' up and down like I just did!"

Everyone laughed and Papa looked impressed.

The thin man closed the oven door and showed them the strong hinge and latch, but Ellen's eyes were on the "Home Comfort" spelled out large and clear in shiny nickel.

He showed them the copper reservoir that could never

rust out—right next to the fire box instead of over on the other side like most stoves. "No sense using leftover heat to warm water when it can come firsthand from the fire-box—right?"

"Good point," Papa said and Mama nodded. "Twice the size of any reservoir I ever saw," Papa said.

"Hey! I'm supposed to be selling this stove!" the thin man said, laughing unnecessarily long and loud. "Always say, 'A good product sells itself.'"

Papa cleared his throat. "How much is it?"

"Sixty-nine dollars, sir," said the thin man.

"Tell you what," Papa said, knocking the ashes out of his pipe against the wagon wheel, "it's just about dinner time. Might just as well have some dinner with us and my son here'll take care of your mules."

They accepted the invitation without an argument and kept up a lively conversation all through the meal all about what was going on in a world far beyond the German settlement.

They were still eating when Papa said he and Mama wanted to take another look at that stove. Mama came back smiling and Papa said, "Well, you can go off lighter by one," and everyone cheered and Papa went to get his money.

The thin man whipped out a bill of sale and wrote it out with a flourish. "Gave you a discount for the meal and the feed for the mules," he said, handing Papa the bill.

"You fellows are smart to come this way in spring," Papa said, carefully counting out the money. "Only time of the year anyone has money is after the log drive."

When the new stove was standing proudly in its place, the men climbed back on the wagon and everyone waved good-bye like they'd been invited guests.

Papa showed Mama the bill-of-sale as they walked back to the house.

"Eighty-nine cents," she read, "for food for men and mules. Now where do you suppose he came up with a figure like that?"

Papa laughed. "Same place he came up with the one for sixty-nine dollars, I guess."

The steam hissing out of the tea kettle brought Ellen back to the present. She poured some hot water into a pan and got some rags. She could still see Mama's happy face that day. Maybe Mama remembered that day, too, whenever she polished it so lovingly.

Ellen pulled out the ash pan, put the rag over her finger and dipped it in fine ashes and polished the "Home Comfort" letters until they shone like silver. She stepped back and admired them and went to work on the nickel trim on the warming oven.

Five more days. She'd tell the girls all about Dr. Pearson. My, that seemed like a long time ago. She'd say, "You never saw such white, soft hands—strong though, and ever so gentle." What if they asked why Mama had to have a doctor? Ellen's eyes glistened with excitement. What a story! "Mama almost died, you know. It was just awful. Dr. Pearson told Papa there wasn't anything more he could do and sadly shook his head. And when he left he looked at me and told Papa he sure was lucky to have a capable daughter like me. Poor man! He probably thought I'd soon be taking over the household." That might be a good spot to hesitate—walk away maybe—blink back tears and then go bravely on—or maybe it would be better to not say *a thing* for a day or two. That would really get them! Just go around with eyes downcast—mysterious-like! She mixed vinegar and salt to scrub the copper reservoir. Phew! She hated that odor.

"Ella! What on earth are you doing!" Mama yelled so loud Ellen jumped, spilling vinegar and salt all over her shoes and the floor. "Look at that clock! Half past eleven.

The boys will be in any minute and you haven't even started dinner." She sat down out of breath and close to tears.

"I'm sorry, Mama. I got so busy polishing the stove. . . ."

"Use your head, girl! People have to eat! Well, I never. . . ." She pounded the table so hard the unwashed breakfast dishes bounced. "Look at that. Dishes aren't even done and you didn't even mix the bread yet." She pointed to the yeast bubbling over the bowl and running onto the table. "*Ach*, I could just . . ." Her voice broke and she got up, trying to sop up the yeasty mess. But before she finished she sank into a chair and burst into tears, just as the boys tromped in.

"What's going on here?" Al bellowed, coming toward Ellen with such anger in his eyes she was afraid he might hit her.

Ellen backed toward the pantry. "Al, don't get mad. I was cleaning the stove and I forgot. . . ."

A small body hurled itself against Al's legs with such force he staggered. "Don't you hit my Ellie!" Gertie screamed.

Little Roy flung himself into Mama's lap howling, and John stood wide-eyed behind Fred who was hastily clattering dishes into the dishpan.

Al took Mama by the arm. "Come on, Ma. Get back to bed." He led her toward the bedroom and shot a glare at Ellen over his shoulder.

After dinner Fred stayed in and dug into the heaping dishpan while Ellen mixed the bread. "You're lucky Pa wasn't home. Can't ya tell time?"

"Cut it out! I don't need you on my neck, too. Think Mama'll tell Papa?"

Fred shrugged. "Maybe she'll forget about it if you work real hard this afternoon."

"How come I can't ever do anything right? All I was

trying to do was get a lot done for Mama so she wouldn't have so much work next week. She says I can go back to school Monday!"

"That's just swell! I know what *I'll* be doing next week."

"I'll help all I can and I'll get up early and I'll come right home from school. . . ."

"Sure. Sure. Anyway, housework beats barn cleaning." He dried his hands and reached for his coat. "Hey, we got some cute kittens in the barn. Come down and see 'em when you get time."

Later when Mama sat up she gave Ellen a few terse orders and then ignored her.

"She *is* going to tell Papa!" Ellen whispered to the flour barrel.

Sleigh bells! Ellen's pulse raced and she ran to put coffee on to cook. Papa would be so cold and hungry!

"Half past three. Pretty good time at that," Papa said when he and Len stomped in and dumped the herring keg and some boxes on the table.

"I helped, didn't I, Pa?"

Papa nodded and smiled at Mama. She hid her smile. Ellen could just imagine how much help ten-year-old Len had been unloading those heavy pieces of bark.

Len munched bread and jam and Papa warmed his hands on the hot coffee cup.

"Plenty cold, I bet," Mama said, joining him at the table.

"Naw. It wasn't cold, was it, Len?"

Len just grinned—with his mouth full.

Papa chuckled and turned toward Mama. "Bet that boy ran more'n halfway there and back. Kept warm while he was running, anyway."

When Len finished eating he leaned against the pantry door and watched Ellen put bread dough in tins. "Papa gave me fifteen cents, and I went to the store and bought a piece of cheese and a whole comb of honey. Was it good!"

Papa heard him and nodded toward the boxes. "Brought a couple combs. Put 'em away for breakfast, Ella. Honey don't go so good with herring."

With one eye on Mama, Ellen unpacked the honey, crackers, coffee, tea and Papa's tobacco. Mama listened to Papa and asked him about the trip, and Ellen wished she'd tell Papa about the stove-cleaning and get it over with.

Papa pulled out his leather money bag and jingled the coins. "Last cash for a little while, but if what I heard today is true we'll soon have money. There's talk that some outfit's going to buy hemlock logs."

"Well, it's about time someone found a use for hemlock logs. Just pains me to know all that good wood's just lying there rotting because tanneries need bark."

"Bothers me too, but there wasn't anything to do but burn it or leave it rot. Sometimes I wonder—plentiful as trees are, if there won't come a day we'll wish we hadn't wasted all that wood and maybe be sorry we cut down so much woods."

"Not hardly," Mama said, "with miles and miles of woods men haven't even seen yet." She laughed. "That would be like worrying that we might get the air dirty by burning wood."

"Well, I guess I'll rest awhile before supper. That twenty-eight miles felt like fifty-six today."

Ellen held her breath. She could still feel the tension between her and Mama. Now she'd tell Papa and he'd frown and scold her and she'd feel like she could just die. But Mama didn't say a word. Papa stretched out on the couch and Mama went back to bed.

She didn't say a word at supper time, either. Maybe she wasn't angry anymore.

Deep in the night, thirst woke Ellen. "The herring want

to swim," Mama always said after a meal of pickled herring. She'd take a long drink of water and let out an "Ahhh" of satisfaction. Ellen crept downstairs in the dark, drank half a dipperful of water and started back upstairs. Papa and Mama were talking. She stopped and listened.

"Don't know when I've been so mad. Can you imagine? Here it is almost noon, not a dish washed, yeast running all over. . . ."

"*Ach,* she got working on that stove and forgot."

"Forgot! Haven't I taught her anything?"

"She just got interested and didn't watch the time."

"No excuse! What am I going to do if I can't depend on her?"

"For one thing, you've been thinking about it too much—got it all built up in your mind. She's been doing a pretty good job these weeks. Now all of a sudden, you're finding fault and taking your feelings out on her. Sure, you got a right to feel disgusted lying here so long and feeling so weak and sick, but there's no sense takin' it out on her."

Ellen held her breath and lifted one foot, warming it against her leg.

" S'pose you're right. Reminds me of last summer when it rained on the dry hay and you hollered your head off at Al," she said with a chuckle. "It wasn't Al's fault it rained but you had to holler at someone."

Papa laughed. "Sure is easier to see things like that when someone else does them."

Ellen switched feet, waiting to hear if they were done talking. She was about to go back upstairs when Mama said, "Poor girl. She really has been doing well. I'll try to be more patient."

Papa's words rode the tail end of his yawn. "Go to sleep now. You'll feel a little better every day."

Startled by the first stroke of twelve, Ellen lost her stork-

131

like pose, scooted upstairs and snuggled deep in bed as the last "thung" died away. "Bless Papa!" she whispered and slept.

Thursday morning Mama ventured out, gave the school children a cheerful good-bye, predicted new snow before evening and went back to bed. She dragged herself out again when she heard Fred grumbling because he had to set up the wash-rig twice in one week.

"We should've let him do all the scrubbing Monday. Ain't so, Ella? Come here. Let me see your hands."

"They're a little tender yet," Ellen said, displaying several dime-sized spots on her palms, "but I don't think the soap will hurt them today."

That afternoon Mama came out when the little ones were asleep and read the catechism—her lips forming each word.

"We've got a lot of studying to do before confirmation. I want you to let some work go these days and get at it, 'cause you won't have time once you get back to school."

"Why'd we have to learn all that stuff anyhow—and in German yet! We aren't going to be preachers."

"For shame! Might be many times in your life you want to remember a Bible verse or one of the commandments when you don't have a Bible right there handy."

"Oh, Mama. That's silly."

"Don't you get snippy, young lady!" She shook her head. "Just goes to show—no one appreciates what they get easy. Here I am so glad to learn all about the Bible, I could listen to Reverend Voss for hours."

Ellen turned her back to Mama and rolled her eyes in exasperation.

Friday morning Ellen plunged into the work with a smile tugging at her lips. Three more days! Oh, she'd help—work as hard as she could mornings and evenings, but it wouldn't be hard at all compared to being stuck home hour after hour, day after day.

Her smile widened when Mama came out fully dressed and took her place at the breakfast table. Gertie clung to Mama's arm and the young boys grinned, trying not to stare at her dark-ringed eyes. Papa looked like he had just set down a tremendously heavy load.

By the time the children left for school and Mama had helped clear the table, she sat down in the rocker, shaken and white.

"Mama, won't you go back to bed?" Ellen pleaded.

"I will. I will. Got to try to stay up more or I'll never get my strength back."

Ellen went back to work; soon Mama tottered back to bed and crawled in with a groan.

Ellen's jaws tensed and her smile faded. Friday. Saturday. Sunday. How much strength could Mama gain in three days?

At dinner time pink spots burned high on Mama's cheeks. Papa touched her face with the back of his hand and frowned. "Feverish again. Told you to stay in bed a few more days."

Did Papa have to sound so angry at her? Maybe he was more disappointed than angry. Ellen certainly was.

About two o'clock that afternoon, in trudged Mrs. Geber. *"Ach,* such a nice day it is I walk. Your Mama? Still in bed, she is?" She threw off her coat and hurried to Mama's room.

When she came out half an hour later Ellen searched her face for reassurance, but she avoided Ellen's eyes and put on her coat. She hesitated with her hand on the doorknob. "Sick lady, she was. Time it takes yet." She closed the door behind her and her footsteps faded away.

"I've got to get out of here!" Ellen thought as she pulled the fragrant crusty bread from the oven and tipped the steaming loaves out on a dish towel. "I'll run down and

133

see the kittens."

She ran all the way to the barn, lifted the latch and slipped into the warm darkness heavy with animal odor. She waited for her eyes to adjust to the dim light.

"Kitty, kitty, kitty," she called.

Old yellow Tabby rubbed against her legs, and a flash of lighter yellow bounced out of the calf pen followed by a white kitten with a black nose. She picked up the white one. "You funny little thing. You look like you stuck your nose in an ink well." So warm . . . so soft. . . . She held it close to her face and smiled when it purred. Old Tabby stretched out on a pile of hay and the yellow kitten began to nurse—rhythmically working its tiny paws. Ellen put the white one down and it played with its mother's flipping tail before it settled down to nurse. Ellen sat down on the hay beside them. "Oh, you cuties! Babies are so cute!"

"Babies are so cute!" The words hung in the air, mocking her. Not all babies. Not that baby in the wooden box. Huddled in a heap of hay, apron over her face, she let the tears come. Some for the baby, some for Mama wanting so much to feel well again, some for Papa, frowning and so concerned, some for herself in the work-filled kitchen—more for herself missing all the giggling and fun in school and Miss McKinley's smiles of approval, and another torrent because she was so sure the whole bundle of misery was all—her—fault.

It seemed a long while later when she dried her eyes, still sobbing intermittently, and struggled to her feet, taking a moment to stomp her left foot awake. When the tingles subsided, she walked back to the house with her eyes on the frozen, bumpy path. She didn't deserve to see dark trees against blue sky or soft white slopes of fields or glistening icicles. She didn't deserve *anything*.

Gertie slipped down from the rocker where she sat humming to herself and looked up into Ellen's face. "You cryin'?"

"Oh, no. It's cold out there. Makes my eyes water."

Gertie wrapped chubby arms around Ellen's neck, and Ellen pressed her cold cheek against Gertie's warm one. How could someone so little be aware of how one felt—and care? "I'm all right now, honey," she answered —her voice husky, and mustered a smile.

Saturday morning loomed ahead long and gray and trying as Ellen hunched over the stove absorbing its meager heat.

When Mama didn't get up, Ellen went to see if she felt worse. "Mama? Are you all right?" Her eyes looked like black holes in a white sheet.

"I'm all right," she sighed. "Your papa gave orders for me to stay in bed."

"You sure you don't feel worse?"

"I'm not worse. Just so blamed disgusted." Her voice shook. "Your pa can't spare Fred to help with housework with all the logging to get done before the skidding snow is gone, and I want you to be back in school, and I want. . . ." She turned and hid her head in her pillow. Ellen reached out and gently patted Mama's shaking shoulder a moment, then tiptoed away.

For quite awhile that morning Ellen felt sorrier for Mama than for herself, but as hours went by and she thought more and more about Monday, self-pity crept in. "I'll just die if I can't go back to school," she confided to the flour barrel.

At supper time, Fred told Papa that Mama had said Ellen could go back to school Monday, and that he would have to stay in to help in the house. "We'll see about that," Papa had answered, and Ellen's last hope vanished.

Sunday forenoon Ellen put a big beef roast in the oven and was peeling potatoes, when the dog set up a commotion and someone yelled, "It's Uncle Walter and Aunt Clara and all the kids—even little Anne!"

"Oh, George! Run and get me more potatoes. You kids! Don't hog the meat, you hear? We've got lots of company."

Everyone crowded in and took off their wraps, and Ellen found the table piled with kettles and dish towel wrapped bundles. "It gets so late when we come after dinner," Aunt Clara explained, "so we brought a few things along." She hugged Ellen. "We'll have a regular picnic—only inside!"

Little Anne held baby Rhineholt, who cried because of all the noise and confusion. Seven-year-old Mayme, little Walter and brother Fred stared at Minnie, Ed, John, Gertie and Roy. "They'll get acquainted about the time we're ready to go home," Aunt Clara said laughingly, and went to see Mama.

Little Anne bounced baby Rhineholt to get him to stop crying, and Ellen tried to get Roy to come and see the baby, but he hung on her skirt and peeked at Little Anne occasionally.

"He's got pretty eyes," Little Anne said.

"So has Rhineholt," Ellen answered, and wondered what else to say. She didn't see Little Anne very often and anyway she was so much older—almost twenty.

"I came to stay and help," Little Anne said.

Ellen wheeled around. "You're going to stay? Oh, I'm so glad! I can go back to school. I'll show you where everything is and I'll help you all I can."

"I would have come before, but I had this cough. I want to help your ma. She's kind of like a mother to me, too. I was real little when your ma got married, but I remember when she took care of me." She nodded, as though Ellen doubted her. "I remember!"

Aunt Clara came back to the kitchen, "Anne tell you she's staying?"

Ellen grinned. "Am I ever glad!"

"Not half as glad as your mama is. She sure hates to have you miss school."

Sunday flew by and Sunday night Ellen wiggled with happiness as she thanked God for letting Little Anne come and stay.

On the way to school Monday morning, Ellen had planned to think about how she was going to act and what she was going to say at school, but she forgot about Minnie. All morning Minnie scurried around trying to be helpful, her eager little face radiant because Ellen was going back to school. She really was a sweet little girl and Ellen was too happy to ignore her, so she made an effort to talk to her as they slipped and slid on the icy ruts.

"What's my class studying in geography?" Ellen asked.

"Just started South America and in history they're still on the Revolutionary War and you gotta learn 'Paul Revere's Ride.' You know, 'Listen, my children, and you shall hear of the. . . .' "

"I know, I know," Ellen interrupted. "I learned that four years ago. Only dummies have to learn poems after fourth grade. We hear them every year!"

Minnie giggled. "I try to keep working but when you hear everybody say it over and over and over. . . ."

The wind took their breaths away at the maple hill, and they turned and walked backward awhile until they stumbled and fell. "I know," Minnie said. "You walk backward and I'll lead you and then I'll walk backward and you lead me."

Sometimes, like now, walking backward like silly little kids, it was fun to be with Minnie. They were tired of the game when they reached the last little hill. They pulled up their mufflers and sucked the damp wool against their mouths with every breath. Ellen had forgotten how cold it could be. All these mornings she had been snug and warm while Minnie had struggled alone like this—unless the boys condescended to wait for her when she couldn't keep up with them.

Now they were almost to the path that cut across the school yard. Ellen's toes and fingers were numb, and the wind blew through her coat like it was made of cheesecloth.

Breathless, they stumbled into the schoolhouse, eyelashes frosty, and blinked in the dim light of the hallway.

"Ellen's back! Ellen's back!" someone yelled, and the girls surrounded her, giggling and chattering. Someone unwound her muffler, someone else took her lunch pail and put it on the corner shelf in the rear of the room. Emma Geber hugged her and Emma Ehrlich tried to tell her something over all the din and gave up. Supper hour at home was peaceful by comparison!

Little boys peeked around the coatroom door, and big ones shuffled their feet and grinned. She had never had so much attention. Miss McKinley smiled and greeted her, but Ellen knew she would act casually about her return because some children were quick to dub anyone afforded excess attention "teacher's pet."

Miss McKinley looked so lovely wearing a starched white blouse with a ruffle around the neck. She tried to imagine Mama dressed like that with a skirt around a tiny waist. Somewhere under all those gathers Mama must have a waist! And wouldn't Mama look pretty with her hair piled up high like that—probably with a rat to make it look even higher—instead of pulled tight and flat against her head and wound into a pug.

At noon there was no opportunity to talk to the girls. Nearly thirty pupils in one room left no area for privacy—unless one considered the frigid outhouse, but no one lingered there an extra second these days.

Even the big boys were eager to tell her what had happened while she was gone. One day they had stunned a big rabbit with a slingshot and brought it into the schoolroom, where it regained consciousness. They had a hilarious time chasing it before they put it outside. Another day the boys went so far back in the woods at noon that they didn't hear the bell and were a half hour late getting back. Miss McKinley was so angry she hadn't let them out at noon for a whole week. Ellen had heard these stories from Len, Ed and George, but she listened to them again and laughed appropriately hard. It was *so* good to be back.

When Miss McKinley dismissed them for the day she asked Ellen to stay after school so she could assign her homework. When the door shut behind the last pupil she sighed a huge sigh and smiled.

"Sometimes I think I can't stand the noise another minute," she confided. Ellen felt positively grown-up. It was like being a friend to Miss McKinley instead of her pupil.

"I met Mrs. Geber last week, and she told me how you had taken over like a little mother. Your folks must be very proud of you."

Ellen studied her shoes and murmured a "thank you." If they only knew. . . .

"Now, don't try to get this all done tonight," Miss McKinley said when she had shown Ellen what she had missed. "You'll catch up in a few days."

Frantically Ellen searched her mind for all those well-formed sentences she had prepared to tell Miss McKinley. They were gone! She couldn't even begin. Miss McKinley was smiling, waiting for her to say something. "Thank you," she croaked and headed for the coat room, her footsteps amplified in the empty room.

She slipped and slid toward home, her head swarming with the accumulation of sights and sounds of the first day back at school. Happy thoughts, until she remembered Miss McKinley's comment: "Your folks must be very proud of you." She groaned. They'd be proud of her, all right! "I'm happy for a few hours and then I'm more miserable than ever," she thought. "Maybe if I work harder than ever I won't feel so guilty."

She ran all the way from the maple hill.

As soon as she opened the door, little Roy lunged into her arms and planted a wet kiss on her cold cheek. Gertie tugged at her skirt. Little Anne looked exhausted. Mama was in bed, Anne said.

Mama's room was so dark Ellen couldn't see if Mama was awake or asleep. "Mama?" she called softly.

"Oh, girl! Where were you? You might know we were waiting for you."

"Miss McKinley was giving me my homework."

"Always 'Miss McKinley! Miss McKinley!' I'm telling you, young lady, you get right home after this. You hear?"

"Yes, Mama," she choked.

Mama's voice dropped to a confidential tone. "It's been a hard day. Poor Anne tried so hard, but little Roy wouldn't have a thing to do with her, and she doesn't know where things are or how we do things. And by the time I tried to tell her or show her, I could just as well have done it myself."

"I'm sorry, Mama. I had to get my work. . . ."

"I know. I know. Now see if you can take over without hurting Anne's feelings."

It was a difficult week for Mama, but she did grow stronger. By Wednesday she was eating at the table again and was helping with sit-down tasks by Saturday when Uncle Walter came to get Little Anne because Aunt Clara had sprained her ankle when she fell down the icy back stairs.

Mama thanked her heartily when she left, but Ellen could sense Mama's relief when they were working alone again.

"We'll manage alone now," Mama said, but she didn't look at all confident.

Getting Back to Normal

Winter wore on day by wearisome day, with little to break the monotony but a change in the weather. Mama dragged herself through these days, regaining strength so slowly that Ellen had to compare her present activities with those of the previous week to see any perceptible change.

After school each evening, hand on the doorknob, Ellen steeled herself against Mama's groans, sighs, and scoldings. But even before she had hung up her coat, she was angry at her. Couldn't she at least let a person get in the house before she started bossing and scolding?

But each time she went upstairs she saw the desolate cradle in the hallway. Even though she tried to keep her eyes on the wide pine floor boards, she knew it stood there silently accusing her. She'd change her dress and go downstairs chastened and contrite, determined to ignore Mama's critical remarks and work and work and work!

So far she had thought of no other form of retribution, but she hadn't stopped trying. Perhaps she'd still find some other way to ease her conscience.

At school, cheerfulness broke through in spite of her martyrdom. She chattered and giggled with the girls, and never did get around to telling them about Mama—nor did she ever again consider unburdening her guilty conscience to Miss McKinley. The risk of losing Miss McKinley's esteem was simply too great. She resolved, quite dramatically, to carry her secret to her grave, work as hard as she could to help Mama and always put her desires second to others' welfare.

Her resolve to deny herself, while certainly sincere, was about as effective as a resolve to stop dreaming. Over and over she failed, and guilt heaped itself upon guilt. Habits, like finding joy in little things, were hard to break. Time and again she caught herself enthralled with a pink and mauve sunset instead of helping Mama cook supper, or became engrossed in the Sears Roebuck catalog instead of her work.

It was just such a moment, about three weeks after she had gone back to school, that Mama stopped to look at the catalog over her shoulder and yelled so loud Ellen jumped. "Ella! Sit still!" Mama peered down at Ellen's head and turned her toward the dim lamplight. "Lice! You have head lice!"

Ellen ran to the mirror. "I couldn't have! I can't see any. Oh, Mama, are you sure?"

Mama nodded, "Ed. Get me the kerosene can. Ellen, undo your braid," Mama ordered, filling a pan with water and putting wood in the stove. "We're going to need a lot of hot water. Minnie, get me some soft rags."

She tore the rags in small pieces, draped an old towel around Ellen's shoulders and began parting Ellen's hair. "Hurry up with the kerosene!"

144

"Here, Mama," said wide-eyed Ed. "What're ya gonna do?"

"I'm going to get rid of *lice*. That's what I'm going to do!" She poured kerosene in a dish, dipped the rag in it and rubbed the length of Ellen's part, made a new part half an inch to the left and scrubbed that one. On and on she worked—parting, scrubbing, parting, scrubbing.

"Ouch, it hurts. Do you have to do it all over? Won't they just smell it and die?"

"No siree! Those little buggers can hide *so* good!" She scrubbed another section. "Boys! Get that reservoir filled and the tea kettle too, and empty the slop pail."

"What in thunder?" Papa growled, sticking his head into the kitchen and sniffing. "Emma! Is that kerosene you're putting on her?"

"It is! That's what my ma used to use on us to kill lice."

Papa shrugged, and sat down to watch the process.

"Please, Mama? I can't breathe. They can't be alive when it's killing me!"

"You just shut up. I ain't half done yet."

"Papa! Tell her to stop," Ellen pleaded.

He ignored her. "Where'd she get head lice? In school?"

"Where else? You been using anyone's comb?" Mama asked.

"No."

"Wearing anyone's cap?"

"No, Mama! My eyes! I can't stand it!"

"You want lice running around? How'd you get 'em? You got any idea?"

"Well . . . we have been combing our hair at noon to see how we'd look with it up like Miss McKinley's—you know—with a rat under it."

"With a rat under it. Whose rat?"

"Ah, ah, one of the girls brought her sister's rat."

145

"*Ach Mein Gott!*" Mama exclaimed. "I bet it was crawling with lice."

Papa scowled. "What's a rat?"

"A wad of hair. Women save their combings and make these wads and wear them to make their hair look high and full." She gave a furious scrub. "You foolish kid! Didn't you know it could be full of lice?"

"What's so bad about lice?" Eddie asked. "I see 'em on the kid in front of me all the time."

"You're next!" Mama said.

Papa caught him by the suspenders as he tried to get away. "Sit down and wait," Papa ordered. He saw George and Len peeking around the doorway grinning. "What're you two laughing at? Get in line!"

"Look here," Mama protested. "I'll have all I can do to get the girls done. You better start on the boys. Comb 'em with the fine-tooth comb and if you see any nits, scrub 'em with kerosene."

When Mama had covered Ellen's entire scalp with kerosene she got out a big bar of brown soap, dunked Ellen's head in the pan of water and scrubbed while Ellen howled. Gertie stood in the corner behind the door holding her ears, and little Roy hung on Mama's skirt and wailed. Minnie tried to lure them into the front room.

"Get them ready for bed, Minnie," Mama said. "I'm going to be busy for awhile."

"My hair's gonna fall right out," Ellen moaned between dousings.

"No, it won't. Someone bring me more water. Keep it coming." She poured water over Ellen's head, sniffed it and soaped it once more, ignoring Ellen's sobs. Again she rinsed it and finally wrung the long hair in her hands and wrapped it in a towel. "You get in there by the heater-stove and dry it good," Mama said, and sat down looking exhausted.

Papa straightened up and rubbed his back. "Ed's all right."

Ed hit for the stairs like a mouse for a hole. No sense taking any chances.

George and Len checked out clean and so did Minnie.

An hour later everyone was in bed except Ellen and Mama. Ellen's hair was still damp. "Shake it out over the stove. You can't go to bed with a wet head or you'll catch your death of cold."

Ellen huddled over the stove. Red blotches burned around her hairline and her eyes were swollen to mere slits.

"Here, sit down," Mama said. Ever so gently Mama rubbed the long hair with a dry towel and combed out the snarls. "How I remember my ma getting after us girls like this. I know how it feels but there just ain't any other way."

Up in bed a little later, Ellen could still feel Mama's hands conveying all the tenderness she was unable to put into words.

The next morning when Ellen looked in the mirror she yelled, "I can't go to school like this. What am I gonna do?" Her hair stood out like a brush.

"Let's try a little petroleum jelly," Mama said, rubbing a dab between her palms and smoothing it on. "Now brush it in."

The results were less than spectacular but Ellen went to school, hoping her cap would help make it lie down. But when she took off the cap her hair flew up like fur on an angry cat.

"What happened?" Emma Ehrlich squealed.

Ed popped out in front of Ellen. "Mama scrubbed her hair with ker . . ." Ellen spun him around and shot him a glare that would have stopped a charging bull. He gulped and disappeared.

"Just washed it, that's all. It'll be all right by tomorrow," Ellen said, wetting her hands in the wash basin and smoothing it down.

All day Ellen knew little boys were snickering and big boys couldn't bear to look at her. It was a bad day.

By the last Sunday in February Mama still lacked energy and often sat down with a groan, but the younger children had forgotten she had ever been sick.

Ellen hadn't forgotten, but it became increasingly difficult to punish herself. There were times when she completely forgot those awful weeks and she enjoyed life like nothing had happened.

This Sunday was one of those times. It wasn't a church Sunday so the day flowed leisurely by. Papa didn't rush out to feed stock after dinner, and Mama seemed content to sit at the table awhile and just talk.

The talk about neighbors began when Papa asked Minnie to pour him another cup of coffee.

She marched around the table with the coffee pot and Al laughed and said, "Hey, Pa, who does she look like hikin' along with that coffee pot sticking straight out in front of her?"

Papa, Mama and Fred all said it at the same time. "Grandma Denker." They laughed and the younger children looked puzzled.

"Don't suppose you younger ones remember her hiking by with that coffee pot," Papa said, tilting back his chair and propping one knee against the table. He took a long draw on his pipe before he continued. "We were still living in the old house. Denkers were building the house they live in now, and it had to be at least four miles between the old place and the new one. Well, instead of the men taking a lunch with them in the morning, Mrs. Denker would carry dinner to them that whole four miles with that coffee pot stickin' straight out in front of her just like Al said. Made your wrist ache just to look at her."

Mama's apron bounced up and down as she chuckled. "Can you imagine carrying that coffee pot four miles, Minnie?"

"Never could figure out why she didn't carry coffee in a pail," Papa continued. "Had to heat it up over the fire when she got there; could have heated it in a pail just as well." Papa hoisted little Roy up on his lap. "Heard tell she used to carry a fifty-pound sack of flour clear from Ogema—that's a good fifteen miles from their place."

"She don't weigh much more than a hundred pounds herself," Mama said.

"Ya, Emma, you're bigger than she is," Papa teased. "I should save the horses and let you carry the flour."

Minnie looked startled and then smiled when she saw Papa wink at Mama.

"I tell *you* that little woman can work," Al said. "Last fall when I worked for them digging potatoes she picked up two rows to my one and every time she passed me she gave me a dirty look!"

"Grandpa Denker always stops and talks and even gives us kids apples," George said, "but not Grandma Denker. She'd sooner sic the dog on us."

Ellen played with a ringlet of Gertie's hair. "Don't you wonder how people like Mr. and Mrs. Denker ever happened to get married? They're so different."

"Don't know how the Denkers met," Papa said, "but you'd be surprised if you knew the stories behind some couples. Take the Herman Hahns for instance. He'd bought a team of horses way down in Mosinee. Well, be danged if those fool horses didn't run away." Papa lit his pipe and everyone waited silently for him to continue. "Well, those blamed horses went clear home to Mosinee, just like Herman figured they might have. He hightails it down there, and sure enough that's where they were—right back with the widow he bought 'em from. Seems like it was just supposed to happen 'cause he and the widow had sort of taken a likin' to each other when he bought them horses. She wasn't bad to look at, good cook and had two fine strong daughters. Yep! Herman got his horses back and ridin' right behind them was his new wife and two half-growed daughters."

Everyone laughed and little Roy, who had been dozing, started, sighed and snuggled down again.

Papa lowered his voice. "At least he had better luck getting a wife than old Crazy Herman out in Town-of-Hill. Couple a years ago I met him comin' out of the post office cussin' to beat sixty, and when I went in old C.B. the postmaster was laughing fit to die. Seems that Crazy Herman had ordered himself a real pretty wife from the Sears Roebuck catalog for six dollars and fifty cents, and all he got was the coat she was wearing in the picture."

At the explosion of laughter Little Roy's eyelids quivered but he slept on. About the time everyone was done laughing someone would start again and they'd laugh all over, until no one really remembered why they had been laughing in the first place.

When the laughter subsided Minnie said, "Papa? Why'd they call him 'Crazy Herman'?" The boys burst out laughing and Len laughed so hard he fell off the end of the bench and rolled on the floor.

Papa frowned at the boys when he saw Minnie was near tears. "That ain't so funny." He turned to Minnie. "You see, out there in Town-of-Hill they've got so many Scandinavians with the same name they have to give them nicknames to tell 'em apart. Let's see . . . there's Pretty Herman and Little Herman and of course Crazy Herman, and their last names are all the same." He smiled at Minnie and she blinked back tears and nodded.

"Well, time to get feeding, boys," Papa said. "Ella, put this fella to bed."

Ellen tucked little Roy in bed, wishing Papa could have talked on and on.

That evening Mama was mixing yeast with potato water (the water potatoes had been boiled in) for bread baking Monday morning. She sighed and said, "Always feel lonesome Sunday night. Tomorrow everyone will go back to school and to work, but I'll still be here listening to the little ones jabber and the fire crackling and the pot boiling."

"I've got an idea, Mama. Why don't you invite Mrs. Olafson over some afternoon?"

"Hadn't really thought about it. I suppose I could."

"Wouldn't it be nice if you two could get to be good friends and visit back and forth?"

"I got more to do than *Kaffee Klatsch* all the time! Anyway, she has Mrs. Benson. They're sisters, you know."

"I know they are." Ellen stopped washing dishes a moment. "You don't like Mrs. Olafson, do you?"

"I don't dislike her—exeept when she lets her fool turkeys fly over my garden fence and don't do nothing about it."

"Oh Mama, that was way last year."

"Sure, but just you wait till I got nice tender lettuce; they'll tear it out just like that!" she snapped her fingers.

"Len could tell her you'd like to have her come over. He goes over there nearly every day—or Guy comes here."

"I'll think about it."

The following Wednesday when Ellen came home from school, Mama was clearing the table wearing her second-best dress.

"Mrs. Olafson just left," she said, sagging into a chair.

"She was here? Did you have a good visit?"

Mama nodded, leaned forward on her elbows and massaged the back of her neck. "It was nice to talk to her, but I just ain't comfortable. She don't understand the German ways and I don't understand the Norwegian ways. At least we had a good laugh over her Guy and my Len walking with those silly stilts. We can't figure out why they want to make walking harder than it is. Found out we'd both been watching them walking on stilts down in the rocky pasture by the creek."

"They have a lot of fun together."

"I know. Well, that was one of the few things we had in common. Thought I was saying the right thing when I said the Norwegian and Swedish languages must be a lot alike. 'It is *not*!' she said, and looked real offended." Mama made a futile gesture. "I just don't know what to talk about with her."

Mama finished clearing the table and Ellen helped herself to a piece of fresh *Kuchen*. She went upstairs to change her dress, feeling disappointed. She had hoped so much that Mama would find a friend.

The next evening Ellen was reading in her room before Minnie came up to bed when Al knocked on her door. He leaned against the doorway with his arms folded and spoke so softly Ellen had to strain to hear him. Al always spoke softly—unless he was angry—sort of like he was talking to his shirt front. He looked concerned and a little worried.

"What's ailin' Ma? She still sick?"

Ellen shook her head. "What do you mean, sick?"

He scowled. "You don't even see it, do you? Too busy flying off to school and thinking about your squealing girl friends and giggling about boys to see how she drags around. Twice now I came in during the day and found her crying."

"You *did*!"

Al chewed his lower lip and nodded. "Think it's still 'cause of the baby?"

Ellen swallowed hard. "No doubt."

Al disappeared when Minnie came singing upstairs.

Long after she heard Minnie's breathing become steady in sleep, she stared into the darkness. "Oh, Mama! How could I forget so soon?"

She rolled and twisted trying to evade the black guilt hovering over her. It wasn't enough to work hard. She had to do more. Maybe Mama would feel better if she could blame *her*. If she poured out the whole awful truth. . . . She sought solace under the covers. There was only one thing to do—tell Mama exactly how she had felt. Mama'd just have to understand. She'd find a time when everyone was out—no, she'd say her throat was sore and stay home from school a day. The very thought of missing school pained her but she had to do it. She slept fitfully.

It took her a moment to define the cause of the sick lump in her stomach the next morning. She renewed her vow. Yes, that's what she'd do. Mama *had* to know what had happened so she wouldn't feel so sad. She'd tell Mama her throat was sore. But she couldn't today—not spelling bee day! Tomorrow's Saturday. Next week. Next week for sure. But now she'd work like everything. She jumped out of the cozy bed into the icy room.

She was buttoning her coat when Mama clapped her hands and looked around the kitchen in delight. "Will you look at that! Dishes done, floor swept, little ones dressed —I've got no excuse for not getting things done today!" She beamed at Ellen and coughed and swallowed like she always did when she found it difficult to say something. Ellen hurried to the door, hoping to get out before Mama said anything but the words followed her through the open door, heaping guilt upon guilt . . . "I just don't know what I'd do without you, Ella."

Her throat ached. Tears threatened. She couldn't stand it. Mama thought she was so good. Monday. Monday she'd stay home and tell her everything. Surely Mama loved her enough to forgive her. But what if she hated her? Mama certainly had a right to hate her. Ellen felt sick all through singing class, and as she reviewed words for the spelling bee and thought of the coming excitement she felt only a stab now and then when she thought about Monday.

The sun shone warm on her back as she walked home from school feeling elated, as she always did, when she won the spelling bee. She tried to concentrate on Minnie's babble but she was trying to think how she would feel some day if she *didn't* win. They were almost to the maple hill when they saw Mama, Gertie and little Roy coming to meet them.

Gertie ran ahead and flung herself at Ellen. Little Roy tried to follow, fell headlong in the slush and howled. Mama set him on his feet, brushed him off and ignored his crying. "Had to get outside awhile," she called. She looked so happy squinting into the bright sun. "Will you look at how high that sun is getting," she said when they met. "A few more days like this and we won't have much snow left."

Mama outtalked Minnie on the way home and even in the house she talked on and on about spring plans, her eyes sparkling, her steps springy.

Upstairs Ellen hugged herself in delight. Mama was fine! All she needed was sunshine and warm weather. No need to stay home from school. No need to tell her about. . . . She whirled around the room in a gay little dance, feeling like she wanted to hug the whole world.

A lot of water ran downhill Saturday in the March sun, aided considerably by Mama and her stick-dug ditches.

She had gone out to feed the chickens and when she didn't come back in the usual fifteen minutes Ellen looked out of the east window to see if she was coming.

Gertie heard her laughing and came to see what was so funny.

"See, Mama likes to play too," Ellen said, putting her arm around Gertie. They watched her and giggled. Mama looked so funny seriously digging ditches with a stick— her *Kopfe Tuch* flapping in the breeze.

They scooted away from the window when she tossed the stick on the wood pile and came whistling up the path.

Fresh air swirled around her even after she shut the door. "My land! I've been out there over a half hour. I start draining puddles and I'm like a little kid—forget all about the time. Always feel like I'm really doing something when I get rid of all that water." She washed her hands and dried them on the roller towel while Roy hung on her skirt. She swooped him up. "Won't be long 'til my little boy can go out and play in a nice, dry yard," she said, blowing down his neck to make him giggle.

It was times like these Ellen felt her love for Mama bubble up like a kettle of jelly about to boil over. Even though her eyes were black-hollowed and her face pale, her eyes were *shining* again! Ellen wanted to run, to whoop and yell like a six-year-old. If it were warmer and dry she'd run across the pasture, scramble over the boulders nimble as a fawn while killdeers flew low—their metallic sounding "killdeer, killdeer" echoing from the hills. She'd laugh at the mother killdeer, fluttering and flopping away from her nest in a dramatic, frantic effort to divert Ellen's attention from the eggs lying on the bare ground. "Bird, you are stupid to lay your eggs right out in the open. No wonder you have a fit if anyone comes near!" she'd tell it.

"Ella! Stop daydreaming and get those potatoes fried."

A glob of lard in the black iron frying pan, melting, melting, like the last bits of ice in the pasture puddles. Covered now by an avalanche of peeled, boiled potatoes, waiting to be chopped with the sharp edge of a baking powder can. Chop, chop, chop. "I'll never fry potatoes when I get married. Never, never, never." Make rings with the can—interlocking rings all around the outside of the pan. Chop, chop. . . .

"Ella! Stop playing games and help me!"

"Yes, Mama." Later. Later, she'd think about spring again. No pangs in her stomach now. She ate more supper than she had in weeks.

Minnie dried a plate, dish towel corner precariously close to the floor.

"What're you smiling at, Ellie?"

"Oh, I was thinking of how the ground smells on the south side of the house when the snow is gone and little green sprouts poke up next to the house."

"And Mama covers dandelions with paper boxes to make them grow faster for salad."

"And robins wake us in the morning, and you can look right out of the window at the green leaves instead of seeing frosty glass."

"I like to hear the robins in the evening. It's like they sit there and wait 'til the shadows get just so long and then decide, now it's time to say good night, and they all start singing at once."

"They sure do! And then when it's almost dark and they're quiet, all of a sudden one goes 'cheep! cheep! tttttttttt!' like she's scolding her little ones saying 'sleep, sleep, tomorrow's another day!' "

Was Minnie hearing the same imaginary chorus of robins, Ellen wondered, as they lay in bed that night? In her dreams she walked through ferny, sun-dappled woods on an endless trail.

Cabin Fever

"It's only the second week of March," Mama reminded Ellen and Minnie as they grumbled about the new snow. "You had better forget about spring for a few weeks."

They watched the snow whirl around the corner of the house in glum silence, hoping Mama was wrong.

But she was so right. Winter didn't relinquish its hold until the last week of March, when the sun shone high and warm, converting ice and snow into slush and water in a few short hours—as though it were no effort at all.

Then with the last Monday of March came the first real evidence of spring, when Eddie came home from school, grinning as usual, with his hands behind his back.

"Got something for ya!"

Mama dried her hands on her apron. "Well now, what on earth . . . ?"

His hand shot out, nearly poking her in the eye. "Pussy willows! Got 'em in Olafson's swamp. Floyd said I could," he added quickly seeing her face.

He hitched himself up on the bench behind the table, propped his pixie face in his hands and watched Mama stroke the pussy willows with her forefinger.

She filled a glass jar with water and said, "Ahhh! The first sign of spring!"

Gertie tugged at her skirt. "Lemme see! Lemme see!"

"See," Mama said holding them lower, "they're just like tiny gray kitty cats." She snapped one off and handed it to Gertie.

Ellen took one, too, and caressed her cheek with it. Gertie petted hers with a pudgy finger, tickled her nose with it, probed her nose with it and pulled it out—fuzzy no more.

What a face Gertie made. Ellen stifled her laughter as Gertie pattered over to the slop pail and dropped it in with a tiny plunk.

Mama doled out fresh bread spread with butter to George and Len, who grabbed theirs and slammed the door behind them, to Minnie who shared hers with little Roy, to Gertie back admiring the pussy willows, and to grinning Eddie.

"I figured you'd like 'em," Eddie said.

Mama nodded and smiled, then turned and exchanged amused glances with Ellen. Only Eddie could grin with his mouth full and still look appealing.

Ellen savored the moment.

Mama pressed Eddie's head against her skirt an instant. "I certainly do like them." She smoothed his hair and looked up at the clock. "My goodness, look at the time! You had better get at your chores."

He scampered off amply rewarded.

Mama sighed and said, more to herself than to Ellen, "Whatever will I do when I run out of little boys to bring me pussy willows?"

Like a candle extinguished by a gust of wind, Ellen's inner glow vanished and a bitter pang replaced it. Because of her one little boy would never. . . .

George and Len burst in the door. "Come see the new lambs! Twins!" George yelled.

"Yeah! Ain't that somethin'? The first time and it's twins!" Len yelled over his shoulder on his way back to the barn.

"Guess we'll just have to take the time to see them," Mama said, reaching for little Roy's coat.

Ellen carried little Roy, and Mama held Gertie's hand while Minnie ran on ahead of them. Roy clung to Ellen in the dark barn until his eyes adjusted to the dim light. Then he chortled with glee when the ewe stuck her nose through the pen and munched the clover hay Mama offered her.

"Clover makes good milk for her babies," Mama explained. She chuckled. "She'll need lots of milk. Just look at those two little fellows!"

Gertie tried to reach in and pet them, and pointed to their silly tails jiggling like dangly ropes as they nursed. Ellen wondered if Gertie would notice that their tails were missing when Papa clipped them in a day or two.

"They've got wobbly legs!" Minnie said.

"They do, all right," Mama said, "but when you remember that they're only a few hours old, isn't it surprising they can stand at all? Think how long it takes for a human baby to learn to stand and walk."

Fred came and leaned on the pen to watch them awhile, then slipped into the pen and picked one up, bringing it out so they could pet its nubby little back and velvety nose. Little Roy tried to poke its shiny eye, and the ewe watched disapprovingly.

The next evening Mama told Minnie and Ellen to run and see the lambs for a few minutes before they helped her with supper.

Minnie ran ahead of Ellen and came tearing back. "Something's the matter with one."

Ellen ran to the barn with her. The ewe stood in the corner of the pen and one lamb nursed contentedly, but the other one lay in the opposite corner with its legs stretched out straight and stiff.

"Come on, little lamb, get up!" Minnie urged.

"You wait here," Ellen ordered. She climbed into the pen with one eye on the ewe and leaned over and touched the still lamb. She gave a little cry and stepped back. It felt like it was filled with plaster. She saw its dry dull eyes—a piece of hay sticking to one of them. "Go find one of the big boys!" she said, trying to control her voice.

Minnie ran out of the barn. Ellen shuddered and scrambled out of the pen. When Minnie came back with Al she tried to control her trembling legs.

"It's dead, all right," Al said. "It just happens sometimes." He squeezed Minnie's shoulder. "Better go back to the house."

Ellen guided the sobbing Minnie out of the barn, but they turned to look back in time to see Al pick it up. It came up in one rigid piece like it had no joints.

Mama listened sympathetically, but when the girls sat and stared at their full plates at the supper table she scolded them. "I know how you feel, but you have to realize life doesn't stop because one little lamb died. You still have to eat."

"You listen to your ma," Papa said. "Settle down and eat and forget about it."

They managed to eat a few bites.

That night before they went to sleep Minnie cuddled closer to Ellen. "All I can see is its legs stickin' straight out. Why did it have to die, Ellie?"

"I don't know. I just don't know why." She hugged Minnie. "Isn't it a good thing the ewe has the other one?"

"Oh, yes! She won't miss it quite as much." Comforted, Minnie slept.

Sleep eluded Ellen for a long while, and when she did doze she dreamed she saw Al lift the stiff white form. At first it was the lamb but when she looked again she saw, not bumpy wool, but white flannel—with blue feather-stitching on it. She turned away afraid to look, yet wanting desperately to see it. When she turned back Al was walking away. She called for him to wait but he kept walking. She had to see it! She tried to run. She ran and ran but he was always far ahead of her.

Her eyes flew open. Night. Rain pounded the window and wind moaned around the house. She dried her wet face on the quilt. What had she been crying about? Her heart thudded in her ears. She jumped out of bed and stood by the window, not daring to close her eyes lest she see the fearful thing in her dream. She shivered and wrapped her gown close around her as a sharp splatter hit the window. Even with her eyes open the dream took shape again—the feather-stitching close enough to touch. A sob rose in her throat. Somewhere out there in that wet and cold and darkness . . . she dove back in bed and hid under the covers. Eventually she slept.

She woke puffy eyed and feeling groggy. Only the thought of Miss McKinley's smile made getting up bearable. She combed and braided her hair and let it fluff out around her face. Encouraged by damp weather, it curled in front of her ears. Why, she looked pretty! She ran downstairs and called a cheery good-morning to Mama.

"*Ach!* What is this?" Mama said when she came out of the pantry and saw Ellen's hair. "If you don't look like a little tramp! Hand me that brush and get over here."

"But, Mama! It looks pretty!"

Mama grabbed the brush, yanked Ellen over to the nearest chair and pushed her down. "I'll fix that hair of yours!" With harsh strokes she pulled every last hair flat against Ellen's head.

Papa came in.

"Don't know what this young lady's trying to be but she ain't getting away with it. Came down here looking like a little tramp if I ever saw one."

Papa just frowned.

Ellen's scalp stung and her ears burned where Mama scratched her, but her dignity hurt worst of all. She clenched her teeth to hold back angry words and slammed carelessly through her work. No mother could treat her own flesh and blood like this. Now she knew. No wonder Mama'd never talked about her birth like she did about the other children. All she'd ever heard was that they lived in Phillips when she was born. How come she didn't have a deep dimple in her chin like the others? How come they named 'Al' after Papa but they didn't name her 'Emma' after Mama? No wonder Mama hated her wiry hair. It wasn't like Mama's. She wasn't like Mama—because she didn't really belong to her—that's why!

Stomach churning, mind whirling, she had difficulty keeping her mind on her studies. She could just see how it must have been. One day they had opened the door—and there she was—wrapped in an old gray blanket—little arms waving helplessly, wailing with hunger. "Why, the poor, little thing!" Mama had said and gathered her into her arms. "We'll keep her, of course!"

Papa surely had agreed. There could never be too many children to suit Papa.

Before she opened the door when she got home that evening, she visualized it all again. She tried to blot out the scenes by looking very hard at the elms, black as ink drawings against the sky down along the river. Fear knotted her stomach and grew to panic. If she hadn't been born to them they owed her nothing and she owed them everything. Her own flesh and blood might be able to forgive her selfishness, but foster parents who had taken her in out of the goodness of their hearts—could they forgive? Her knees felt weak. She wanted to run away and hide in the woods.

She jumped when Mama rapped on the window and beckoned to her, and when she stepped in the house Mama's words felt like physical blows.

"Come in here and get to work!" Mama shouted. "The older you get the less help you are. There you stand just gawking around when I need. . . ."

Ellen slung her coat over a hook and ran upstairs before Mama had finished. "I was cute—babies are so lovable—but now, now she hates me," she muttered.

Grudgingly she worked beside Mama that evening, speaking only when spoken to.

She was putting the last of the dishes away in the pantry when Mama came in and said, "Something bothering you, my girl?"

Ellen shook her head.

"Never mind," Mama said, lifting Ellen's face with her hand that smelled faintly of yeast, so that Ellen had to look at her. "We all have times when the whole world seems wrong. You'll feel better tomorrow." The smile she gave her made tears spring to Ellen's eyes.

Quickly as she could she ran up to her room and sat in the dark, thinking and thinking. She'd been so sure all day today that Mama hated her, that she was a foundling. But now—that smile. Tears rolled down her cheeks. How could she know for sure? Ask Mama and Papa, "Was I born to you or did you take me in?" Hardly.

She lit the lamp and stared at herself in the mirror. Did she look like them or didn't she? The longer she looked the more undecided she was. Someone else would be a better judge of that than she was. That's it! She'd ask Miss

McKinley tomorrow. She'd have to be very careful so she didn't suspect something. Maybe if she asked, "Do I look more like my mother or my father?" That might do it. She shivered. What if Miss McKinley said, "Why, to tell you the truth, I don't see any resemblance to either one of them—I guess you just look like *you*." She heaved a huge sigh. That was a chance she'd simply have to take.

The opportunity came when all the children were outside at noon recess. "Miss McKinley, do you think I look more like my mother or my father?" Her heart thumped so hard she was afraid Miss McKinley could see it right through her dress.

Miss McKinley studied her face for a small eternity. "Well, Ellen, I can see both your mother's and your father's features. You don't have your mother's deep-set eyes. Your eyes are more like your father's. You don't have the deep dimple in your chin like your father, but there is something about your smile that is very much like his. Your nose is exactly like your mother's."

Ellen had heard enough. Hastily she mumbled thank you and ran toward the coat room. She heard Miss McKinley call, "Why did you want to know, Ellen?" but she pretended not to hear her.

Outside she leaned against the schoolhouse wall, weak with relief. Surely it had all been her imagination.

She wasn't so certain when Mama began scolding the moment she walked in and scowled at her like she hated her. When she spilled some sugar, Mama carried on like the sugar was gold dust. Mama was yelling so loudly she didn't even hear Papa come in, or look up and see him take Ellen's arm and lead her to the front room.

Papa shook his head, but to Ellen's surprise he was smiling. "Your Ma's got a bad case of cabin fever, that's all that's wrong with her." He winked at Ellen. "I'll take her for a buggy ride and get her out of the house a little while. Shoulda done that a long while ago. You be able to manage here?"

Ellen nodded and grinned.

"Emma!"

Mama jumped. "Oh! You startled me. I didn't even hear you come in."

"No wonder, the way you were yellin'."

Mama blushed.

Papa took the dish towel out of her hand. "You've been cooped up here all winter. High time you got out a little while."

"Out? Whata you mean 'out'?" She stuck out her chin defiantly. "You tell me just where I might go at this time of the day?"

"I'll take you for a buggy ride."

"A buggy ride! At this time of the day when there's supper to cook and. . . ." She shook her head. "If I didn't know better I'd think you'd been drinking. Never heard of such a thing. Go traipsing out at this time of day."

"Now what's wrong with going for a buggy ride when you feel crabby?"

"Oh, so I'm crabby, am I! Well, sir, if you had to put up with all this. . . ."

"That's what I'm trying to tell you. Come on. Get your coat. Ain't a thing here Ella hasn't done alone these past weeks."

Mama peered out of the window. "It is awfully nice and clear out. . . ." She reached for her old blue *Kopfe Tuch* but Papa took it out of her hand. "Here, wear this." He handed her a pink gingham sunbonnet that had hung all winter on the same hook. "You look real nice with something around your face."

Obediently she tied it, trying not to look pleased, and slipped her arms into the coat he held for her. "Now, Ella, you see that. . . ."

"Never mind!" Papa interrupted, guiding her firmly out the door. "She'll do all right. Forget the house. Forget supper. Forget the whole darn works!"

Ellen was too busy distracting bawling Roy from the window to see them leave, but a few minutes later she caught a glimpse of the buggy bumping up the hill toward the maples, with Mama sitting primly on her side of the seat.

The little ones were playing so contentedly when the dog barked about an hour later that they didn't even run to the window. Ellen looked out in time to see Mama sitting practically on Papa's side of the seat. He held out his arms and she stepped down into them, and he whirled her to the ground. She took a step in the direction of the house but Papa pulled her back, gathered her in his arms and kissed her—and kissed her again. Ellen's heart flip-flopped. Honestly! Married people acting like lovers! Papa was still holding Mama close and she was *enjoying* it! Her arms clung high around his neck like she never intended to let go. How embarrassing! Like opening a door and seeing someone bathing. Ellen felt that she shouldn't be watching and yet she couldn't tear her eyes away. Finally Papa released Mama, but she leaned against his rough coat while his big work-hardened hands moved gently over her shoulder blades, as if to soothe all the tiredness away. It must be wonderful to have strong arms around you—to have a man shelter you—kiss you like you were infinitely precious. And yet, it was not quite decent. Was it? Why, she felt a strange sensation—in the most unlikely place! Her face burned. She'd never thought that Mama might *want* to be close to Papa. Oh, she knew people *had* to be in order to have babies—but that was what a woman *had* to do if she wanted babies. It was one of those things about nature that had to be done—like going to the outhouse. But this—seeing them together like this. . . . She felt dizzy. She knew Papa and Mama loved each other, although she rarely saw them touch each other. They laughed together, planned together, worked together—but she had never thought about them being together—*this* way! It seemed so natural now for two people to want to be close—like the time she had wanted to be close to Henry. She blushed to think of it. Just a few weeks ago when the ice was good on the river, they had been skating. Henry had picked her up when she had fallen, and had supported her unnecessarily long. She still remembered the power of those blue eyes drawing her closer and closer with an irresistible force. Nothing in the world existed but his face and wanting to feel his lips on hers. Closer, closer—she thrilled at the memory—and didn't Al give them a shove, and Henry skated away to catch him. She had stood there feeling so cheated—she'd wanted to pound lumps on Al!

Oh, my goodness! Mama was almost to the door! Ellen fled to the pantry. Mama would see her flushed face and know she'd been watching!

"Ella! Where are you?"

She took a deep breath and came out. "Have a nice ride?"

Mama had her back toward Ellen, hanging up her coat. "Oh, yes. So clear we could see the mill smoke way down at Tomahawk." She turned and a shock shot through Ellen. Mama's usually pale cheeks matched the pink sunbonnet she was untying, and her eyes glistened like a child at Christmas. She smoothed her hair, gave herself a little shake, and settled her face into a concerned-housewife frown—but her eyes still glistened.

Log Jam

Mama's birthday! Ellen ran most of the way home April eighteenth so she could bake Mama's birthday cake before supper. She had just put the sugar in the mixing bowl when Mama came in from feeding chickens.

"Oh, dear! Now it will start again—wet socks and overalls and underwear all over the place," Mama said as she hung up her coat and sat down dejectedly. "Pa heard they're getting ready to blast the ice jam at Squaw creek, and you know what *that* means!"

Ellen shook her head.

Mama scowled and gave her a well-where-have-you-been-all-your-life look. "When the ice is out the log drive starts. You know that, for goodness' sakes." Mama got up and broke a dry leaf off a geranium and twirled it in her fingers as she stared out the south window toward the river. "Every year I dread the drive a little more."

"But, Mama! Remember? You were as excited as the

rest of us last year when they had to blast that big jam just east of the old house. At least something *happened* around here for once."

Mama sighed. "I know. I know. But I'm so afraid someone's going to get hurt. Those boys! I know very well they'll build a raft this year like they always do and ride when the water is high. One careless moment is all it takes. No matter how much I warn them they'll take chances, and I. . . ."

"Oh, Mama. They never get hurt."

"There's always a first time." She gave the fire a vicious poke. "I'm so relieved when the sackers poke those last stray logs downstream and the drive is over for another year."

Ellen beat the cake batter until her arm ached, rested a bit and beat it some more. Couldn't Mama just think about how exciting it would be? If something happened—it happened. What good did it do to worry? Golly, these next weeks would be fun. Wait 'til the boys heard about the drive. Their chores would get done in a hurry and they'd hightail it down to the river. Ellen couldn't recall a year when the boys (first Al and Fred, now George, Len and Ed) hadn't dragged a few choice logs out of the river and put them together with a couple of old boards and a handful of nails. The resulting raft, while admittedly no work of art, was the source of enough thrills to last the boys many a week. Every night, after the logs had gone down for the day but the water was still high, they'd ride it down river and drag it way back up again, hiding it up on a bank under alder branches. Quite likely the river men pretended not to see it, but at the end of the drive when the sackers scanned the banks for maverick logs, it had always been found. All that ever remained were the boards, just where they'd landed when the sacker's well-aimed blows had sent them flying. Far down river somewhere the precious logs bobbed along, on their way to join thousands of others in the Wisconsin river. Maybe this year. . . .

"And another thing," Mama continued, "if your Papa and those boys think I'm going to stand for having my floors clomped full of holes with those cork-soled shoes, they got another think coming. Sure, they tromped all over the old house with them, but they ain't getting away with that in this house. Caught them hiking in a couple times last year, and they probably think I'll forget all about it this year. She sighed, "These next weeks will be awful."

Minnie hung over the cake bowl trying to swipe a fingerful of batter. "How come they call them 'cork' shoes when they got nails stickin' out of 'em?"

"Beats me. Guess 'calk' is the right word. We just always said 'cork.' Means spikes, I suppose." Mama smiled. "Can't you see those men riding those logs with smooth soles?"

"Especially Mr. Wieglet!" Ellen said, and she and Minnie giggled.

"Now, girls. Shame on you. You shouldn't laugh. At least he tries. Got to give him credit for that."

George and Len burst in the door and dumped wood in the wood boxes.

"My cake!" Ellen wailed, and yanked open the oven door.

"Oh, for goodness' sakes," Mama said. "It hasn't been in there long enough to even start to rise." She sharpened her little knife on the edge of an earthenware bowl with a whit, whit, whit, whit and yelled, "I want you boys to. . . ." She looked up at the open door. "Well! Look at them go!"

They were running toward the old house to beat sixty. Small wonder they were curious. Men were carrying sacks and crates and barrels into the old house.

"Wonder what's going on," Mama said, and shut the door. "Something to do with the log drive, no doubt."

Stealing frequent glances out the window, Ellen helped cook supper. It seemed like hours before Papa and the big boys came in and explained that the old house would be used for a cook shanty during the drive. But that wasn't all! Fred had been hired to work as cook. He was exuberant. His very first job! Al would work on the drive with Papa, as was expected. Ellen wondered if Fred's elation was entirely due to the prospect of earning money. Fred had never expressed a dread of the cold water and treacherous work of the drive, but he didn't enjoy boisterous activity or the challenge of physical accomplishment like Papa and Al did. No, Fred would gladly work with the cook, high and dry above the tumultuous river.

No one even remembered it was Mama's birthday. She looked forlorn while the log-drive talk flowed around her. Her eyes brightened when Ellen brought out the cake all covered with whipped cream, and the attention turned briefly her direction as Papa teased her about getting to be an old lady. The talk swung back to the logs again.

"Hey, Fred, you gonna give us cookies and stuff? We'd carry water or something," Len bargained.

"You kids just stay away. You just stay away. Ma! Tell 'em to leave me alone or I'll lose my job."

Mama shook her finger at the row of them. "All of you stay away from the old house. If I hear that you kids are bothering Fred you won't get out of my sight!"

Papa frowned. "You mind your ma. If Fred needs help he'll ask for it." He tilted back his chair and the frown eased away. "Ran into Big Jim Delaney about noon. By golly, that man must save up energy all year long. Couldn't steam along like that all year. Like to know how many miles he's hiked this spring already. Says he's hired over fifty men from Spirit Lake to Spirit Falls." Papa unwound his legs and got up from the table. "Lots of snow this year. Should be high water this spring."

"Sure hope so," Mama said with a sigh. "Higher the water the shorter the drive."

"Women," Papa snorted. "Always worrying!"

"I'm never going to worry like Mama does when I have a family," Ellen muttered to herself as she cleared the table. "I'll *enjoy* things."

Like a gleeful schoolboy, Papa strode in the door Thursday noon and yelled, "The drive's on! They're blasting Squaw Creek first thing tomorrow morning."

Fred and Al let out a whoop and Al thumped Fred's back, and swore without thinking.

Papa glowered at him and Al wilted. Papa wasn't a swearing man and didn't see any reason his boys had to be either.

"It wasn't that bad a word," Al said close to Ellen's ear, and gave her apron string a quick yank.

She took her time tying it, sort of hoping Papa would see Al had untied it and yell at him again. Al thought he was so *smart*. Would serve him right! But Papa was too busy heaping his plate with steaming mashed potatoes to notice anything else.

Saturday morning Ellen had no trouble finding something to look forward to. She planned to work as fast as she could and get down to the river, but by eleven she knew she'd never get down there until after dinner. She shot Mama's back a glare. "She's just dreaming up jobs so I can't get down there," Ellen grumbled to herself.

It wasn't 'til they were washing dishes that Ellen had any idea when Mama'd consider the work done.

As though she had just thought of a brilliant idea, Mama said, "Why don't you take John down to the river and I'll bring the little ones later when they wake up?" She smiled and watched Ellen's face expectantly.

Ellen clattered a pile of plates into the dishwater and didn't relax her hours-old frown one bit.

"Well! Fine how-do-ya-do. Thought you'd be glad to get down to the river. Can't see what you got to pout about." Mama went off shaking her head, and Ellen rolled her eyes ceilingward and groaned.

Ellen made quick work of the dishes, then wiped all the crumbs off the table onto the floor instead of carefully into her hand, almost wishing Mama'd catch her doing it. "Come on!" she snapped at John, shoved him into his jacket, threw on her coat and half dragged him across the yard. Even before they started down the hill behind the barn they could hear the logs thudding and men yelling.

"Look at that water!" she yelled as they caught sight of the river. "Look at 'em come! They musta just opened the sluice gate!" It must have taken all morning to build up a head of water like this. She hadn't missed much, after all.

"Johnny, look!" she screamed over the roar and swept him up in her arms so he could see farther. Logs careened around the river bend, some shooting up on shore, while the white-water men hopped from log to log with peavies breaking loose any log that stuck before it could form a jam. There came Johnny Mitchel riding as comfortably as could be. Papa said he was the best white-water man on the river. It looked so easy, but the less agile men seemed to be in the water more than on the logs.

She put John down, and they ran downstream and watched three men tend out logs from the river bank with long poles when they caught at the bend. Any log that didn't move could cause a jam.

Logs and more logs—as far as they could see. Well behaved, most of them, content to bob along midstream but, like headstrong cattle, a few sought the slightest opportunity to cast themselves up on shore, or cling to a rock or a bush.

And so it would be, here on the river for at least two weeks, until all the logs decked along the river had thundered down the rollways and splashed into the icy water—except during the night when the sluice gates were closed so the water would rise high enough to float another riverful of logs the following day.

John tugged at Ellen's sleeve. "Are Papa's logs in there?"

Ellen nodded.

"They're gonna get lost!" he wailed.

"No, they won't. I mean it doesn't matter. The company scaled them at the rollways. They know how many Papa had."

He looked up at her, nose wrinkled. "Logs don't got scales?"

"No, silly! Not scales like a fish. This kind of scale means measure—count."

If it wasn't so hard to yell over all this noise, she'd tell him how Papa stamped the end of each log with a stamp hammer bearing the company mark, and that he cut a watermark about six inches from the end, so no one could cut off the end of the log and change marks without making the log conspicuously short. He'd learn all that—eventually.

The logs dwindled. For a moment the men downriver didn't notice. Then the cry went up. Jam! Jam!

Ellen grabbed John's hand and ran upstream. They met Minnie.

"Come on! We can see from the bluff!"

River men running upstream brushed past them. One said, "You stupid kids. Get outa the way!" But another one grinned over his shoulder as he ran and said, "Hey there, young man. Gonna be a white-water man someday?"

John looked startled and grinned back.

They hurried up the cork-tracked trail across the pasture, up past the old house and on up to the bluff where they huddled together in the chilly wind and waited, wide-eyed. Logs and more logs barreled down with the rushing water and crashed against the jam, while men dodged and leaped in their frantic attempt to dislodge the key log. Ellen hardly dared to breathe. Logs slipped under the jam; others veered off to the sides, missed men by inches and sent up great splashes of water. Some struck with such force they upended and crashed back into the water. Ellen felt like her heart would stop its furious pounding, like a rabbit shot at full chase, if a careening log suddenly hit one of the men. She strained to see through the sheets of splashing water. Were Papa and Al down there, or were they working upstream on a roll way?

She grabbed John by the coat collar and held tight as they leaned over the bluff.

"Quit chokin' me!" he hollered, wiggling out of her grasp.

She wrapped an arm around him and felt his heart beating like a frightened bird.

And still the jam grew—like someone had dumped out a whole box full of gigantic match sticks. By now the men had stopped rolling in logs from the nearest rollway when someone had run and told them to hold up, but on other roll ways farther upstream logs continued to roll in. It would take a little while to spread the word upstream.

"Hope they hafta blast," Minnie yelled.

John quivered with excitement. "I wanna see 'em blast! I wanna see 'em blast."

"Don't be silly," Ellen scolded. "We couldn't see it anyhow. They'd chase us out of here."

She hardly dared to blink now. Deep inside her she wished the logs would pile higher and higher until it was the biggest jam anyone had ever seen, but then a stern voice chided her—told her she should be ashamed of

176

herself for wanting the jam to build when so many lives were at stake. "But it's fun! It's exciting. Nothing exciting ever happens around here!" she argued. Before it could chide her again a chorus of yells and cheers went up. Men scrambled up on the banks while logs broke loose in a twisting, tumbling roar, and swept furiously downstream. Men ran full speed to head them off at the bends, and Ellen took a tremendous breath of delicious cold air and let it out with a whoosh.

Minnie ran down the trail but John stood glowering at the commotion below.

She shook his shoulder. "Come on! What's the matter with you?"

"I wanna see 'em blast!"

She yanked him down the trail with her, and he stumbled along reluctantly 'til they saw Mama waiting with Gertie and little Roy. He broke away and ran to meet them yelling, "We saw a *big* jam! We saw a *big* jam!"

At first Ellen thought Mama was crying. No . . . she was *laughing*! Mama pointed to a man out in midstream trying to heave himself up on a log. He flopped up on it like a wet seal and attempted to stand. Frantically his arms and legs flailed the air, and down he splashed between the bobbing logs. It *had* to be Mr. Wieglet. Most men with his lack of agility stayed safely on shore and tended out logs at the bends. Not dear old persistent Mr. Wieglet. Perhaps he knew how much tension he dispelled with his hilarious efforts, or maybe each year he dreamed of gliding effortlessly along accompanied by cheers instead of laughter. At any rate they were all laughing too hard to notice a rough-looking man stride out of the brush toward them. He shook his fist right in Mama's face. "If you think it's so blasted funny, *you* go try it!"

His red and black plaid mackinaw disappeared before Mama could pull her chin up off her chest. Her face flamed. "It's a mighty good thing your papa didn't hear him speak to me like that!" she said with a toss of her head. Then she lowered her head to hide a smile. "Can't really blame him though. It's hard, dangerous work and here we have the nerve to stand and laugh."

Sunday afternoon Emma Ehrlich and Emma Geber came over. The three girls linked arms and sauntered along the river bank, assuring each other they looked years older with their braids pinned up, and laughed at the way they had run helter-skelter last year with their braids flying.

"Darn these short skirts," Emma Geber said, looking down at the expanse of black stocking between her coat hem and shoe tops.

Emma Ehrlich scooted over to a log and sat down with her coat and skirt over her knees. "See! They don't show sitting down!"

"Well, we can't *sit* all afternoon!" Emma Geber snapped.

"Oh, what's the difference," Ellen said, tilting her head to one side. "I think you'd look older if you held your head higher. Yes, that helps. You look *much* older." She whirled ecstatically. "Wait 'til you see all the fellows! There's some real good lookers!"

They chose a spot and settled themselves above a sharp bend—skirts draped over black stockings, heads high and practiced the disdainful looks they would bestow on any young man who dared to speak to them. The effect, they hoped, was natural enough to convince anyone that Sunday afternoons were commonly spent on the river bank in this fashion. Meanwhile, they chattered incessantly.

"Too bad your folks didn't name you 'Emma.' We could be 'The Three Emmas,' " Emma Ehrlich said.

Emma Geber shifted to a more comfortable position. "Funny they didn't. Oh well, your ma'll probably have a little 'Emma' one of these days. After all," she said with a giggle, "every family has to have an 'Emma.' Ain't so, Emma?"

A sick feeling shot through Ellen's middle. There'd *never* be a little "Emma Verleger." She turned away.

"Why, Ellen," Emma Ehrlich said. "I didn't know you felt bad about not being named 'Emma.' "

Ellen gulped and gave herself a little shake. "Let's go upstream."

They began to run, burst out laughing, assumed their young-lady roles and strolled up the path.

That night Ellen's face burned in the darkness of her room when she thought of that silly act. Mama would disown her for sure if she knew how they'd pranced up and down that river bank, picking spots where the men almost had to fall over them to get past. She hid her face in her pillow when she remembered how they'd actually run giggling into the woods when a young man with bushy black hair had winked at Emma Ehrlich.

Of course they had acted sensibly when George and Len came in sight and they never did see Papa or Al—but what if the boys had seen them carrying on? They wouldn't dare tell Mama and Papa—would they? Ellen shivered when she thought how Mama would react. Mama had enough worries these days. She knew the boys were riding their raft just as surely as she knew it was useless to forbid it. She'd yell, "You be *careful,* now!" each time they ran off, returning to her work with furrowed brow. Ellen suspected she kept in constant communication with God— no doubt imploring Him to delegate a special contingent of guardian angels for the duration.

That week Ellen saw little of the river activities. Too much work. After supper the second Sunday of the drive she joined Minnie up on the bluff to watch the boys ride their raft. John clamored for a ride, so she took him down and had him sit on it so he wouldn't fall off. He came back with his bottom dripping. "Oh, my gosh! I might have known the water'd slosh up between the logs," she groaned. "Now I'll have to take him home and I hardly got to watch at all."

"I'll take him home," Minnie offered. Ellen gave her a quick thank-you hug.

The boys were daring her to ride when a movement upstream caught her eye. She screamed, but before the boys could move, a dozen or so logs, probably broken out of a small jam, hurled down upon them. She hurled herself down the steep bank as the logs hit the raft and the boys flew into the churning water. George and Len were already crawling up on the bank when she reached the river's edge.

"Where's Eddie?" she yelled.

They looked around. No Eddie.

"Over there!" George yelled and pointed to Eddie's hand clinging to the raft, lodged at the first bend. Eddie was wedged between the bank and the raft.

Her legs wouldn't move fast enough. Mama was right! Sooner or later someone would be hurt. Maybe he was even dead! Not Eddie! Not little Eddie with the big grin. She was the oldest one there. She should have had sense enough to know how dangerous it was—and here she was encouraging them!

Her legs trembling, she slid down the muddy bank and grasped Eddie under the arms. George and Len plunged into the water and pulled the raft away from the bank, while she tugged Eddie's limp body up on shore. His eyes rolled back 'til she could see only the whites, and his neck was limp as a dead bird.

"He's dead! He's dead!" she sobbed.

George put his ear to Eddie's chest. "He ain't dead. I can hear his heart real good. See! He's breathing."

She struggled to see through her tears, and started when

a man wearing a red and black plaid mackinaw loomed over them. Good heavens! The man who had shaken his fist at Mama!

"Move over. Let me see!" he ordered.

Why did it have to be *this* man of all people? She tried to control her trembling knees and waited for him to start scolding.

The man examined Eddie with deft but gentle motions. He beckoned to Ellen. "Come closer. He'll be scared when he comes to and sees me."

Ellen knelt so close she could smell the heavy tobacco on his breath.

Eddie's eyelids quivered.

"He's coming to. Talk to him!"

"Eddie! Eddie!" she choked. "It's all right. Ellie's here."

He blinked, gasped and opened his eyes. His face contorted in pain. "My legs! My legs!"

The man took off his mackinaw and carefully laid Eddie on it, then pulled off Eddie's stiff, wet overalls as gently as a mother. "Wiggle your toes, son."

Eddie wiggled them. "Feels like my legs are broke off right below the knees."

The man eased up Eddie's long underwear legs and exposed ugly red welts on his thin white legs. Ellen was sure they grew larger as she looked at them.

"Anything else hurt?"

"My head—in the back."

"He got a nasty blow," the man said, examining Eddie's head. He turned to Ellen. "Mighty lucky. Nothing broken. Bad bruises. He'll hurt a few days. Where you kids live?"

Three hands pointed north.

The man scooped Eddie up like he was made of straw and grinned at scared, shivering Len and George. "Looks like you fellers could stand some dryin' out." He hiked up the bank and took the path toward the old house. He walked so fast the three half ran to keep up with him.

George pulled Ellen back. "We can't let him carry Eddie in—Ma'd be scared as anything. Let's have Len run ahead and let Ma see how wet he is. She'll be so busy hollering at him she won't even notice us and we can get him upstairs."

"Why, George Verleger! You don't want Mama to know 'cause you might have to give up your precious raft! You oughta be ashamed of yourself. Eddie coulda been killed."

"*You* oughta be ashamed of yourself. Wait'll I tell Ma how you was carryin' on down by the river last Sunday. I saw you sittin' there makin' eyes at the guys and giggling and runnin' and trying to get 'em to notice you silly girls."

"You *wouldn't*!"

"Wouldn't I?"

"You threatening me?"

"Why, Ellie. I wouldn't think of *threatening* you. It's just a bargain. Best part is we both win."

"No, sir! I'm not letting you kids get hurt or even killed."

"All right. Have it your way. It's my duty to tell Ma and Pa how you been carryin' on, or hard telling what kind of a girl you'll turn out to be."

Ellen panted along, one eye on the man ahead of them. They were nearly to the cedar swamp. Not much time left.

"Another thing," George panted, "we already had an accident. That means there's less chance of having another one. Right? We'll see that one of us watches for logs all the time, too."

Ellen groaned.

Len slipped back and grabbed Ellen's arm. "P-please, Ellie. We'll be awful careful. We only got a few more days."

"All right! All right! But you gotta carry Eddie to school tomorrow if his legs hurt and carry him down to the river and do his chores . . ."

"Sure! Sure! We figured on doing all that. Hurry up. Let's catch the man and tell him."

They had to run to catch up with the man and had to keep running to stay abreast of him.

"Mr. . .," she puffed. "We're awful glad you helped us and everything, but we don't want you to carry him in the house 'cause our ma'd be so scared if she saw a stranger . . . bring . . . him . . . home. Could you just . . . take him . . . as far as the woodshed?"

He nodded. "Guess you're right. Wouldn't hurt none to give him a little brandy. 'Course your ma'll know what to do—see that he gets good and warm and everything."

At the woodshed Ellen pulled off her coat. "Here. You take your coat. It's just a few steps. I won't get cold."

George took Eddie from the man's arms. "Thanks. Thanks an awful lot."

He pulled on his coat, damp as it was, and wheeled around and was gone.

Len was nowhere in sight.

They stopped at the door—heartbeats thudding in their ears. They grinned at each other. Mama was hollering like everything.

"You dare complain! Oughta turn you over my knee insteada feeling sorry for ya. Got a good notion to keep you in the house 'til the drive ends."

"That ain't fair! I wasn't the only one that got wet."

"Are you telling me what's fair? Before I know it you'll all be down with pneumonia."

"You just don't want us to have any fun. You never do!"

Ellen winced. "Now he's gonna get it!"

"Let's go!" George whispered. He made a beeline for the stairs when Ellen opened the door.

Upstairs, Ellen piled quilts on the shivering Eddie. "George, you have to help me get the brandy. Let Mama see how wet you are, and while she's yelling I'll get a chair and get the brandy bottle from the top pantry shelf."

It worked. Mama was still yelling at George when Ellen held the bottle to Eddie's lips. "Just take a tiny sip," she ordered.

He gulped, choked and gasped. Ellen thought he'd never catch his breath. It set off a coughing spasm and Ellen heard Mama yell. "See, I told you. Whole bunch of you'll get pneumonia yet. Listen to that boy cough."

Ellen clapped her hand over her mouth, fled to her room and laughed 'til she cried.

The next morning, Eddie donned his grin right along with his clothes, but he confessed that he couldn't count the spots that hurt. He kept a wary eye on Mama, hoping she wouldn't notice his limp. As soon as they were out of sight, George carried him the rest of the way to school.

Ellen stayed with the boys on the way home from school. When they grumbled about carrying Eddie she warned, "You'd better shut up. And if you're smart you'll hustle up and get wood and water in. Mama won't pay any attention to who does it as long as it gets done."

They took her advice and Mama didn't even notice that Eddie wasn't doing any chores, but they didn't relax until Saturday when Eddie was off and running again.

Saturday night Papa sat down wearily at the supper table. "Whew! That's that for another year. They'll be sacking the rear another day or two, but Al and I are done."

Ellen saw George, Len and Eddie exchange worried glances.

Mama's furrowed brow relaxed for the first time in days and her body sagged like a slack rope. "Can't tell you how glad I am—and how thankful." She shook her head. "Just too good to be true. No one sick—not even so much as a bad bruise."

Ellen didn't dare look at the boys.

The weather was beautiful Sunday. Much too nice to stay in the house, Ellen thought. While Mama and the little ones napped and Papa and Al rested, she slipped out of the house. She wandered across the field west of the house to a ditch that ran from Olafson's swamp through a culvert under the road, then bisected the field and emptied into the cedar swamp below the hill. Minnie, Eddie and John were too busy with their miniature log drive to notice her. She had an impulse to help them build the dam higher. No! She would *not* squat down in the mud. She wheeled around before they saw her, resisted another impulse to run down the hill, and tripped lightly along as though she wore yards and yards of white ruffles and carried an elegant parasol like the one in the picture she kept tucked away in her dresser drawer. She spread her imaginary skirts over a smooth gray rock, and sat overlooking the river bend east of the old house. Poor old river. It would take months for the rain to wash away the scars of the drive. Its banks had been savagely undercut, and trees leaned precariously into the water here and there. All things heal in time, she told herself as she sauntered up toward the bluff. I certainly am growing up, she thought. I sound just like Mama.

George and Len came trudging down the well-worn path carrying some battered boards. They ignored her. Danged old sackers! They could have left that little old raft, she thought with a surge of sympathy.

From the bluff she could see the spot where Eddie had been dragged out of the icy river. If he had been badly injured—or killed. . . . A shiver ran up her spine. How could she have forgotten! She hadn't even thanked God. She did so now with her head bowed against the rough bark of a huge maple, then started back down the trail toward the old house.

The door stuck and then creaked open as if reluctant to expose the house's deplorable state. A lump grew in her throat as her eyes wandered over the familiar walls—the marks of screw holes where the roller towel used to hang, the streaked windows Mama had kept shining, a rickety old table and some kegs the men had used for seats, one lone cracked glass mason jar on a pantry shelf, and the wood floor, now the color of ashes, Mama had kept white by constant scrubbing with lye soap. The scene wavered through tears. Maybe Papa should tear it down—save it from this humiliating ruin. She couldn't bear to look at it any longer. Chin in hand, she sat on the doorsill with her feet on the flat gray rock that had served as a doorstep for so many years. How many times had she swept it—mud in spring, dry gritty ground in summer, crumbling leaves in fall and snow and ice in winter. Winter. She could still remember how cold the wind felt that day Mama had dressed her and called Al and Fred to take her for a sled ride. They were coasting on the steep slope in back of the house, and were in no mood to tug a three-year-old around. Mama called again and went in the house. A few minutes later they came up the hill, scowled at Ellen, brushed her aside and stomped into the house.

"Ma! Ma!" they yelled in unison. Ellie said nasty things to us. Ellie said we're . . ."

"I heard you," Mama interrupted. She looked from one to the other.

"You're lying!"

"No, we ain't. You should hear her, Ma. Honest! You think she's such an innocent little baby girl. You oughta hear her!"

Mama yanked her in, pushed the boys out, pulled down her bloomers, and the boys must have heard Mama's hand smacking her bare behind even above her screaming. Mama jerked her clothes in place, warned her that this was a mere sample of what she'd get if she ever said a thing like that again, shoved her outside on this very rock and said, "Now. Take her for a ride."

Out of Mama's sight the boys hovered over her, wiped her tears and hugged her. Fred even kissed her. "We're sorry, Ellie. Honest, we're sorry!"

Al wiped his nose on the back of his hand. "Where'd you like to ride?"

Fred brushed tears off her cheeks. "Wanna go real fast?"

The sound of her own laughter snapped her back to the present. Poor Mama! Those boys gave her some bad times. Like the morning some years later when Mama sat crying. Papa worked in the lumber camp that winter and came home only weekends, and Mama did chores in addition to her household work with the dubious help of the boys.

"The last one out of the barn be sure that the door is shut," she had called to them as she pulled off her overshoes after milking that morning. A while later, when they were ready to leave for school, she heard the barn door banging.

"Who was the last one out of the barn?"

"Not me," Al said. "Fred, you were still in the barn when I came in."

"I was *not* the last one through that door," Fred insisted.

"Oh for goodness' sakes! You *had* to be the last one if you were in the barn when Al went out."

Fred grinned. "Was not. Jumped out of the hayloft window."

"You what?" Mama's voice went up as high as Uncle Hank's violin. She was laughing and crying at the same time, and yelling, "You foolish boy. You could have broken your neck." She settled down for some real crying, while they all stood open-mouthed watching her. "I just can't take it!" she sobbed. "Your pa's just going to have to come home from the woods, and there won't be money for new shoes, or kerosene for the lamps, or flour for bread or. . . ." She sobbed long, awful sobs into her apron. The boys slunk off to school, and the barn door stopped banging.

Ellen got up from the doorsill and leaned against the frame. She closed her eyes and remembered the house the way it had been—bright rugs on the floor, white curtains billowing at the windows, the stoves crackling and the smell of baking bread floating out to meet her when she came home.

It had smelled like bread baking that January day when Papa had sent them all out to play in the thresh floor and told them to *stay* there. She was four that winter—still too small to be content in one place very long. After what seemed like a very long time she slipped quietly back into the house and was halfway across the room when Papa, sleeves rolled up, hands dripping, came out of the bedroom looking obviously startled when he saw her. Angry, too!

"You cat, you!" he snapped in German. "Get back in the barn!"

She ran back and huddled in the hay like a frightened rabbit, staying there until Papa came and said they had a new little sister—which was no big news to her. She'd heard a baby crying when she'd gone in the house.

Papa had picked her up and given her a hug. "Well, *liebchen,* you have a little sister. Her name is Minnie." She was puzzled for a long time. It had seemed so simple— Mrs. Geber brought the new babies. How come this time the baby was crying in there and Mrs. Geber hadn't even come yet?

She chuckled to herself as she walked around the house and scanned the woods up along the river bank, as she'd done so often this spring, for a small mound of fresh earth. The pain was always worse when she hadn't thought about it for awhile. She had almost forgotten the baby these past exciting days. Somewhere . . . somewhere . . . there was such a mound. The old house's site seemed such a likely spot, but the snow had melted and grass was greening on the south slopes and still she could see no mound. She *had* to know where it was, but she could never bring herself to ask Papa. Poor Papa. How had he managed to dig through all that snow and frozen ground and still stay so close to Mama those days. She stood leaning against a towering elm tree for a long time, deliberately remembering those terrible days in January. She had to think about them— make herself remember the terrible thing she had done. What kind of a person was she that she could so quickly forget? She thought about how cute the baby would be now—chubby and soft and warm and gurgling when she talked to him. It felt good to cry again. She felt better about herself just listening to her sobs echo down the river.

Still sniffing, she walked down and dipped her hand in the cold water, splashed it on her eyes and dried her face on her skirt.

As she climbed back up the south bank she found them—three Mayflowers of the palest lavender imaginable. Lovely . . . lovely. She slid her fingers to the very bottom of the downy stems and picked them. All the way home she breathed their faint fragrance. How could anyone feel sad when spring was almost here?

Meeting at the Little Grave

Papa came in from doing chores Monday morning bright-eyed and rested. He whistled as he worked soap suds up his arms and massaged it into his hands, making a squishing sound. "Don't suppose you'd want to ride to Tomahawk with me today, Ella. Pretty chilly yet and the roads are bumpy and. . . ."

Ellen let out a squeal and hugged Mama. "Can I really? Can I really go?"

Mama gave her a quick hug and feigned a frown. "Now, don't get all excited. We got lots to do. Papa's taking the butter so we have to pack that, and fix a good, big lunch for you two. . . ."

Ellen didn't hear her finish. She was thumping upstairs to tell Minnie.

When they turned north at the schoolhouse corner, Ellen still trembled with excitement. Too bad the river road wasn't dry enough to use. It would save several miles.

Over forty miles to ride today. Would she ever be tired of riding? But for now she was blissfully content to ride. She drew in deep breaths of cool spring air and let her eyes rove over the greening fields and wooded hills.

At the crest of Benson's hill she pointed down where a section of roof and the chimney were visible above the trees. "Look at our lazy smoke!"

Papa chuckled. "Does look lazy. You cold?"

"Only my nose. Think it'll warm up later on?"

Papa scanned the sky and nodded. "Sure will if it stays clear like this."

They rode in silence while Ellen searched for something to say. It seemed odd to talk to Papa alone. She discarded a number of ideas and finally said hesitantly, "Papa, what's the first thing you think of when you wake up in the morning?"

"Hmmm, well . . . I guess first of all I think, 'What day is this? What day of the week?' The date don't matter so much."

"You do?"

He nodded. "And then I kinda let my thoughts roll around a little 'til something good comes into my mind, and then I start thinking about that and pretty soon I want to get up and get living."

She bit her lower lip. Held her breath. *Just the way I think when I wake up in the morning. I must have inherited that.* All those thoughts about being a foundling —she *could* be wrong. She *must* be wrong. Goose pimples prickled her arms and she basked in a cup-runneth-over feeling and smiled at Papa. He smiled back—a little puzzled, it seemed—and knocked his pipe ashes out on the side of the buggy seat.

A fresh breeze swept over the last remains of roadside snowbanks and the reviving fields. Ellen loved the smell of sun on damp earth, and wrinkled her nose when a whiff of horse smell mingled with it. The wheels scrunched alternately over gravel and then rolled silently over sand, while the horses' hooves clop-clopped a pleasant rhythm. They hardly seemed aware of the light rig behind them. After struggling with heavy logs all winter, no wonder this buggy felt light.

Papa was as proud of his team now as he had been when he bought them ten years ago from Loeb and Hammel. "Got to get a heavier team," he'd been saying lately. "They're just too light for logging."

Ellen flushed with pride when she recalled overhearing Mr. Stuhl telling some of the men after church one Sunday that Al Verleger could get as much work out of his Kate and Nell, neither one over 1,300 pounds, as most men got out of much heavier teams because he took such good care of them and handled them with such skill. She had been so proud of Papa and wanted to tell him about it, but she never had. It wasn't always easy to talk to Papa.

She rode silently, watching the horses' muscles ripple under shining brown hides. Horses awed her, and she preferred to be no closer to them than she was in the rig—not like Len who worked under and around them and let them nuzzle the back of his neck. Gave her chills to even think about it. Al, Fred and George knew how to handle a team, but it was Len who had a way with them. It had become his job, almost to the exclusion of cow-barn work, to groom and feed them. But the horses held a limited fascination, and she squirmed and sighed. Such a long way to Tomahawk. How could Papa stand to spend so many hours on this road—even in spring?

"Don't you get sick and tired of riding to town?" she sighed. "It takes *so* long!"

"Sometimes. If I'm in a hurry. Otherwise I've got too much to think about." He struck a wooden match under the buggy seat and drew the flame down into his pipe with a sucking sound. "Mighty good time for planning." He tapped his forehead with his pipe stem. "Everything a person does has to start up here, you know. Seems to me the more a person plans the more he does. Like the new barn, for instance, I've got it planned pretty near down to the last nail."

Ellen inched a bit closer to Papa. "What's it going to be like?"

"Well . . . it's going to be at least forty feet wide and eighty feet long, with a hip roof, and a thresh floor in the middle of the barn—at ground level so you can drive right in with a wagon. And doors on both sides so a man can drive right through."

"Golly!"

"And hay chutes—two of them. One for each row of stalls in the cow barn down below."

"What're chutes?"

"Nothing but holes, really—with a trap door. Sure save a lot of work carrying hay. Can throw it right down where you need it. 'Nother thing. The horse barn'll be on the opposite end by the thresh floor, so they'll be right next to the oat bin."

"Gee, that's smart. Did you think of all that yourself?"

"No. No, I sure didn't. Was in a barn like that once when I bought a cow."

"Will it be painted red like in pictures?"

Papa nodded. "Not right away. Costs a lot of money to build a barn that size. Might have to wait awhile before we can paint it."

"You can just see it, can't you, Papa?"

He turned and smiled at her. "Sure can."

For one precious moment Papa had looked at her like a person. Like someone who thinks and someone he enjoyed talking to—not a little girl who forever did things wrong. She wanted to hold onto the moment but he looked

194

away—lost in his own thoughts. She waited. Maybe if she was quiet he'd talk some more. Meanwhile she relived the moment so she would be sure to remember it.

"Got a lot of other things planned too," he continued, and her heart gave a pleasant little leap. "Soon as the barn's built I'm going to add a big kitchen with a milk room and a pantry, and two more bedrooms above it with a concrete cellar under it."

"Gee!"

"And a separate room in the cellar—all cemented, with a drain in the floor so it can be washed down nice and cool for your ma to churn butter in. Oh, I've got a lot of details to work out yet. Hey! Look at that! We're almost to Middlefarm."

"Such a silly name. How come people call this farm Middlefarm?"

"Because Middlefarm Anderson lives there."

"That isn't really his name?"

"No," Papa chuckled. "The way I figure it, Alvin and Langley Stone had a farm at Stone Lake, one at Spirit Falls, and this one—so this was the middle farm. When Anderson bought it, well, folks just started calling him 'Middlefarm Anderson.'"

"People get so used to saying a name they don't even think how funny it sounds," Ellen said, pulling her collar a little higher and wiggling her toes to keep them warm.

They turned south and went down a hill and up another one before Papa spoke again. "Got some plans for you kids, too. One thing I sure do want is an organ for you girls. Al's getting real good with the violin. You and Minnie could learn to chord on the organ and it would sound real nice."

"If Ma don't holler."

"Oh, she only hollered when Uncle Hank used to sit upstairs at the old house, squeaking away and keeping time with his foot when there was a baby sleeping."

"Wish you still had your accordion."

"Always figured I'd buy another one, but I kinda forgot about it."

"Len says he's going to buy you one when he gets big. He felt awful bad about dropping it."

"I know he did."

Papa didn't talk while they bumped and bounced over the stretch of corduroy on the outskirts of Spirit Falls. When the buggy rolled smoothly again, Papa said, "Have to stop and see Hank a minute. Don't go far. We got to get going again."

Ellen didn't like Spirit Falls with all its smelly, noisy saloons nearly as well as she liked Tomahawk, but after seeing nothing but home, school, and familiar landscape all winter even the sight of the smoke stacks made her heart thump. She hunched forward in the buggy seat to catch the first glimpse of the big red roundhouse. Just as it came in view the locomotive chugged across the trestle, sending tremors through the ground and chills up Ellen's spine. It disappeared into the roundhouse, and Ellen waited for it to come back out. When it did the whistle startled her and Papa laughed.

The sounds of the town grew louder with every step of the horses. Ellen could hear the zing of the saw at Bradley's mill to the south and Nick's mill to the north. "They sound like one's trying to outdo the other, don't they?"

"Got a hunch they're trying to outdo the other in more than makin' noise. Listen! Hear Hank's anvil? Every anvil has its own special ring."

Ellen tried to listen to what Papa was saying about anvils but she kept thinking about the waterwheel at the flour mill. If she hurried, she could run down and get a quick look at the pond and the waterwheel.

She was on the ground almost before the buggy rolled to a stop in front of Uncle Hank's blacksmith shop. Down the boardwalks she ran, gathering sights and sounds as quickly as one might gather wild flowers in the wake of a thunder storm.

Papa was sitting up in the buggy when she came running back. Uncle Hank grabbed her braid as she ran past. "Hey. Hold up! Can'tcha even say 'hello'?"

"Hello," she said with a glib toss of her head, and climbed up in the buggy.

Uncle Hank leaned against the door frame, arms crossed high on his chest as they rolled away. "Sure glad the little fellow's all right," he called to them, and went into the shop. He came right back out, cupped his hands to his mouth and yelled, "Hey, Al, bring me five pounds of welding compound."

"What kind you want, Cherry Heat or Climax?"

"Don't matter. Good welder can weld with any kind!" He made a face at Ellen and she made one back, then glanced at Papa. He was smiling. If Ellen had done that to someone else Uncle Hank's age Papa would have scolded her for being disrespectful, but Papa still considered Uncle Hank his little brother and applauded his boyish antics. Of course, Uncle Hank's silly wife did the same thing. Roguish as he was, Ellen knew Uncle Hank had a serious side to him. He had demonstrated that just a minute ago when he said, "Sure glad the little fellow's all right."

Even now, several weeks after that awful Sunday evening, Ellen felt sick when she thought of it. Uncle Hank and Aunt Emma had been visiting most of the day. Aunt Emma was acting silly as usual, and Uncle Hank kept teasing her—oblivious to Mama's frown. The older children sat around watching them like they'd watch playful kittens, and little Roy rolled happily on the floor.

Pretending to grow tired of her pestering, Uncle Hank

shoved Aunt Emma into the hall, slammed the door and held it with his huge boot. Aunt Emma pounded and yelled and finally Uncle Hank winked and gestured that he'd let the door go and she'd come flying through. Everyone watched, laughter ready, but to their horror he stepped back and planted his big boot right on little Roy. Aunt Emma came sailing out and landed on top of little Roy—still giggling.

"Mein Gott! I killed him!" Uncle Hank yelled.

Papa pushed him aside and laid his ear on little Roy's still chest. Aunt Emma's giggles turned to loud sobs. Papa looked up—his face contorted, and hissed, "Shut her up or get her out of here, Hank!"

Uncle Hank pulled her to him and pushed her face into his shirt front, never taking his eyes from little Roy's white face.

Everyone crept closer, breathless and wide-eyed. His lips turned blue and bluer still.

Mama let a sob escape. "Can you hear it? Can you hear it?"

Papa shook his head.

Mama pushed Papa aside. "Let me try." For a moment the only sound was the clock ticking and once the fire snapped.

"I hear it! I hear it!" Mama whispered, pulling up his shirt with trembling fingers. A red welt was rising on his left side.

Papa let his breath out in a shoosh. "Thank God. Must have just caught his side."

Little Roy's face made the shape of a cry, but no cry came. Then his little ribs expanded and he let out a thin wail. Everyone breathed again.

Papa ran his fingers over little Roy's ribs. "Don't seem to be broken but it's awful hard to tell." Ever so carefully Papa lifted him and put him in Mama's arms. She sat in the rocker and held him like he was made of spider webs, gently murmuring to him. He cried a long while and then slept.

Uncle Hank and Aunt Emma didn't go home that night, and Uncle Hank must have leaned over and asked how he was a hundred times. When it was very late Mama turned to Uncle Hank, patted his cheek and said, "Why don't you go to bed, boy? I think he'll be just fine."

A moment later when he passed Ellen on the way upstairs she saw tears on his cheeks. She had wanted to hug him like a hurt little boy.

The buggy was scrunching through gravel near Squaw Creek when she came back to the present. She blinked back tears, glad to see Papa wasn't looking at her.

A comfortable silence prevailed until they reached the first stretch of corduroy. Ellen clung to the buggy seat, braced her feet and clenched her jaws tight to keep her teeth from chattering.

"Want to get out and run a ways?" Papa yelled over the loud bumping.

"I'll try it," she yelled back. "Don't leave me!"

"Whoa!" Papa yelled and the buggy jolted to a halt. Papa leaned over to help her out, but she was over the side. Papa gave the horses a chirp and called over his shoulder, "I'll pick you up on the way back!"

Ellen shook her fist at him in mock anger and began to run. It felt good to leap from log to log and she kept up with the buggy for a few minutes, but then she fell farther and farther behind. Papa didn't stop immediately when the buggy rolled on smooth ground again, but she knew he was teasing her. She had to stop running when a pain stabbed her side. Papa stopped and grinned at her.

"Had enough exercise for awhile, huh?"

She nodded, too out of breath to answer, and accepted Papa's helping hand.

For a while it felt good to ride again. For a while. Nothing but woods, woods, woods, she thought. She sighed and Papa shook his head. "Such impatience! Tell you what. Let's try something. See that tree with the limb hanging over the road like a crooked arm?"

She nodded.

"Keep your eyes on it. Just watch it come closer."

She watched. She became more impatient instead of less. It just didn't *move!* She waited and waited, wondering what Papa had in mind. She listened to the wheels scrunch on stones, the horses clop, clop along and the buggy squeak. So slow. It came closer, closer still and finally they passed under it. She looked at Papa questioningly.

"Took a long time, didn't it? Now. See that nice, round maple tree? Let's see how long it takes to get to it. This time tell me what you see—*everything* you see as we ride."

"All right . . ." she said doubtfully.

What was there to see except the same old woods? "Well, I see those crows up ahead." Three crows were pecking at a pile of horse manure. They fled with a powerful thrust of blue-black wings as the buggy approached. "I didn't know crows were *that* big."

"Listen to 'em caw-cawing like they're telling us we got no business on this road. Pesky devils. Smart, though. Read where a fellow got one to talk. Kept it for a pet."

"I read about one like that. It pulled clothespins off the line, and hid everything shiny it could find, and said 'hello' and startled people."

"Sounds like the same story."

Nothing moving now. What was there to see? "Can't see much now. Lots of colors if you really think about it. There's a real red bush over there and I can't even count all the different shades of green. And the clouds look like rolls of carded wool when Mama lays them on a quilt back before she puts on the top and starts to tie it."

"Never thought of that. They sure do look like quilt wool. Hey! You know what we just passed?"

Ellen turned and saw the maple tree receding behind them. She laughed delightedly. "I forgot all about waiting for it to get closer. Now I see! You get interested in looking at things right around you and you forget you're even waiting for something."

Papa grinned. "A person can do about the same thing when it comes to any kind of waiting. Even if it's weeks or months or years. Keep busy and interested with whatever's right in front of you, and the time will pass before you know it."

Ellen tucked her new insight neatly back in her mind like she'd put a new hair ribbon in a drawer—so she'd know exactly where it was when she wanted it. Then she turned her thoughts to the sights and sound of Tomahawk only minutes away. She felt her pulse beat faster at the very thought. She'd look and look and look—carefully as could be—so she could tell Minnie and the little boys all about everything. And she'd pick out Mama's dress goods like Mama said she could. It had to be something clear and bright with no gray in it at all. Seemed like everything Mama wore was sort of gray. When had she made herself a new dress anyhow?

There was the river! It looked even more broad and blue than she remembered. She wished Mama could see it. Mama loved the blue and green of the water and trees. And the islands. "Wouldn't it be fun to take a boat and go out and see what's on those islands?" Mama'd say when they got to this spot. "Something mysterious about islands. S'pose it's just more trees and grass just like here but I'd like to walk around on one once." Mama liked a boat ride, too. So smooth and quiet, she said—not like bumping along on a road.

They rumbled across the wooden bridge. The Wisconsin

River. Some of this very water beneath them had run past the old house. Sometimes they'd toss cowslips or violets in the river and watch them bob downstream and pretend they'd go all the way to Tomahawk, and on down the Wisconsin River—maybe even to the Mississippi or even the ocean! And sometimes she wished she was so tiny she could crawl into one and go along and see all the wonderful things all along the way. But then she'd suddenly be glad she couldn't, 'cause it would be awfully scary to go that far away from home and everyone.

"You rubberneck like that all day and you'll put your neck out of joint," Papa teased.

Right now Ellen didn't mind that the horses walked slow. She had time to look at the sparkling water. It was still a mile to Main Street, but there was so much to see now she didn't mind. What was it like to live in a house so close to other houses that you could talk from one porch to another? And those tiny yards! It would be nice to have friends so close. But no river to stroll along—no woods and fields? Would Mama like that? Maybe someday she'd get married and live in a house in town and Mama'd visit her. If she lived here she'd dress up every day and put her baby in a wicker buggy and walk downtown. She'd invite neighbor women over for tea and they'd use lovely china —so thin you could see the light through it and . . .

"Tell you what," Papa said, and Ellen jumped. "You can take a walk down to the end of Main Street and meet me back here at Olehafen's store. Just down to the end of the street and back."

"Yes, Papa," she called back as she bounded out of the buggy and started down the street at a trot. Women were staring at her. They walked along with tiny mincing steps. Her cheeks burned and she walked with smaller and smaller steps, glancing out of the corner of her eye at their tight shoes and cinched waists. There was music. It must be coming from a saloon. Oh, how she wanted to stay and listen, but she hurried on without trying to find its source. So much to see—windows full of things she'd never seen before. Splendid watch fobs for gentlemen, and a lady's necklace shaped like a heart with a real diamond in the center, and fancy ladies' back combs and parlor lamps with roses on them. Oh, she'd never remember everything.

She hurried on—afraid Papa would be waiting for her. A young man, perhaps in his twenties, tipped his hat to her like a grown-up lady. My goodness! She must look grown up! Wait 'til she told the girls at school. She drew herself to her full height and took very small steps all the way back to Olehafen's store.

While Papa was buying groceries, Ellen wandered around the dry-goods side and tried not to stare at two elegantly dressed women. Such suits she had never seen! Not a wrinkle at the waistlines. Those waistlines! Surely a man's hands could span them. How frustrating to try to remember the design of the braid trim and the details of the ribbon and flower-covered hats without staring at them. The colors were no problem. One was lavender— deeper than the Mayflowers she had picked yesterday— and the other was the color of cinnamon.

She hadn't had nearly enough time to look at them, when Papa came toward her, suddenly looking coarse and even grimy. He had never looked like that to her at home—but here with all the other men wearing white shirts and. . . .

"Why, hello, Mr. Verleger," said a pleasant voice behind her. Ellen whirled around. A gray-haired lady smiled over the counter at Papa.

"How-do, Mamie. How've you been?"

"Just fine! Just fine! And how is your family and your . . . well! I declare!" She pointed to a tall, thin boy standing open-mouthed by the open stove door, staring at

203

Ellen. "Alvin. Shut that door. And your mouth, too, while you're at it!"

She turned to Papa. "Good worker. Except when he sees a pretty girl!"

Papa cleared his throat and looked pleased. "Ah, Miss Dewing, this is my daughter, Ellen."

Ellen was trying to find something to say besides how-do-you-do when Papa said, "Tell you what. I have to run over to O'Connel's to get some welding compound. Why don't you women pick out that dress goods your ma wants while I'm gone."

"Why, of course," Miss Dewing said, beaming a smile at Ellen. "That's women's business."

Ellen nodded, but no words came. Too much happening too fast. She felt dizzy. First a young man had actually tipped his hat to her, and just now a boy had stared at her, and Miss Dewing had referred to *her* as a "pretty girl," and now she had to decide on Mama's dress goods, and she'd never picked out dress goods alone before, and there were so many—all bright and new-smelling—and she couldn't find a thing to say, and she felt stupid, and . . .

"Just take your time, my dear," Miss Dewing said, like she knew exactly how Ellen felt. She ran her fingers down a pile of bolts. "These are calicos. Eight cents a yard." She leaned closer to Ellen. "But if I were you I'd get percale like those for twelve cents a yard. Calico's only twenty-five inches wide; percale's thirty-six. Here, feel the difference, too—and the percale's fast color."

Oh, they were pretty. At least ten different bolts of percale. When Papa came back Ellen was trying to decide between a myrtle green and white check and an old rose with tiny white flowers. "I can't decide, Papa. Which do you like?"

Papa shrugged. "Take 'em both! Wrap 'em up, Mamie."

If Ellen ever wanted to hug Papa, it was at that

moment. "Won't Mama be surprised?" she whispered. While Miss Dewing wrapped the package, Ellen wandered off a few steps to take a closer look at the enormous oval-shaped stove that took sticks of wood four feet long. Why, it would take up half the front room at home.

When Mamie handed Papa the carefully tied package, Ellen came back to Papa, said good-bye to Miss Dewing and followed Papa out to the buggy. She was about to bounce up into the buggy, but she stood very primly, waiting until Papa loaded some parcels and helped her up. He looked a bit surprised but he didn't say anything.

At first they talked about all the things they had seen, but before they got to Uncle Hank's they had fallen silent—each contentedly reliving the day.

At Spirit Falls Papa gave her a dime to buy candy at Bradley's store, while he and Uncle Hank had a quick glass of beer.

She waited for him to hand her down and she walked off, allowing herself to take steps no longer than the width of two boards in the walk. How could she have run like a ragamuffin just a few short hours before? A burly young lumberjack doffed his cap as she passed, and she lifted her chin and walked on, keenly aware of bosom and waist and vowed she'd never run again—except maybe at home.

She bought peppermints for Mama and chocolate drops for everyone else. Her mouth watered for them, but she waited to eat one until she was seated high up on the buggy seat. Wouldn't be ladylike to go walking down the street with a mouthful of candy.

A mile or so out of Spirit Falls she let her head go ragdoll limp and nod to the rhythm of the horses' plodding gait. Tired. So tired. But so happy. She could see Mama's eyes sparkle when she opened her dress goods and the way she'd smile at Papa.

Then they were on Strucker Road heading into the

sunset. Ellen was only faintly aware of the colors until Papa said, "How'd you like a dress and a hair ribbon like one of those colors?"

"Would I ever! They're awfully pretty. Makes me feel sad, though."

"Sad?"

She nodded. "Hate to see them fade. Wish I could hang onto them somehow."

"Well now, ain't that what makes a sunset so special? Wouldn't be nothing if a person could pull it out of a drawer and look at it any old time. When you see a sunset you know you're seeing something that will only look exactly like this one time. The shapes of those clouds, and that special combination of colors will never be the same in any other sunset. Nope! Never again. Get the feeling, even when I'm in a hurry, that a person ought to take time no matter what and never miss watching a sunset. All too little beauty in life," he said, almost to himself. "No sense missing what there is."

Ellen wanted to tell him she understood—that she'd never, never forget his words. But she knew her voice couldn't get past the lump in her throat.

At home she bounded down from the buggy. No matter if it wasn't ladylike now. She couldn't *wait* 'til Mama opened her dress goods.

"My land. That's a big package. How many yards did you get?"

Ellen ignored her question and watched Mama carefully wind the string, wanting Mama to throw that old string away and get at unwrapping the package. Mama put the string in the drawer of the washstand and opened the paper. "Two pieces! What on earth did you buy two pieces for?"

"I just couldn't decide. They were both so pretty . . . Papa said to take them both."

Mama snorted. "Your Pa! Of all the foolishness! All the things you children need . . . and here he goes and buys goods for two dresses!"

Papa dropped a load of packages on the table. "Aw shucks, Emma, make one up for one of the girls."

"Lot you know. Yardage don't come out right."

"Well, make an apron or something," Papa glanced at Ellen, who was blinking back tears.

Mama scooped up the bundle and took it to her bedroom. Ellen glared at her back. Did Mama *have* to spoil it? Why did she always have to take the joy out of things?

Papa rubbed his whiskers, making a dry scratchy sound, and frowned. Ellen knew he had seen her glare at Mama. She held her breath. His frown melted into a smile. "Don't be too hard on your ma. What she needs is a trip to town herself one of these days." He went back outside and Ellen sighed and unbuttoned her coat, trying to ignore the little ones chattering. She wanted to feel sympathy for Mama—she really did, but a hard knot of disappointment and anger lay deep inside her as insoluble as a stone. She hung up her coat and sagged into the rocker.

"Well!" Mama said brightly, bustling back into the kitchen. "Tell me all about your day. Did you have a good time?"

Ellen pretended to be listening to Gertie as she wavered between nursing her grudge and babbling all about her trip.

Mama kept right on talking. "I just know how tired you are. I always say I get more tired going to town than if I'd cleaned the house from top to bottom." She sighed. "But it's worth it. Person has enough things to think about for weeks. After a trip I can just shut my eyes and see all those pretty things for days and days." Mama's eyes sparkled at the very thought of seeing new things.

Sympathy loosened the hard knot within her. How *did* Mama stand being home day after day, looking at the same old black stove sifting ashes out of its door, the worn chairs with each crack and scratch so familiar one wanted to scream, *"Change,* why don't you!" Everything the same. Yesterday, today, tomorrow and tomorrow and tomorrow. Why, that could be why Mama always talks about the weather! It changes!

The knot had gone away, she realized, and suddenly energy bubbled up from some mysterious source. Ellen bounced to her feet, helping to set the table as a torrent of words poured out.

When the men came in for supper she was still attempting to make the day come alive for Mama and Minnie.

After supper everyone had a chocolate drop and Mama had a peppermint. Ellen had to run and take a drink of water to wash the candy out of a hollow tooth.

"Seems like a week since this morning," Ellen said when they were washing dishes.

"Must be because a person sees so many different things," Mama said. "I feel the same way when I've been to town."

Later, snug in bed, Ellen tried to think over the day's events, but she fell asleep immediately. In her sleep she twisted and turned, trying to escape the torturous confusion of a thousand scenes swirling and blending to the rhythm of Uncle Hank's hammer. If she could run—get away—get away from the pain. Pain. Pain. Pain. Every time the hammer hit the anvil. She tried to run, but her feet hardly moved down the boardwalk in Spirit Falls—no, Tomahawk. Olehafen's store! She'd run in the store and she wouldn't hear it, and the pain would stop. The boy, Alvin, stood by the open stove door. "Get in! Get in!" he commanded.

She peered in at the roaring red coals. "No! No!"

The bed gave a loud creak as she started. She opened her eyes. Dark. Her heart thumped and with hammerlike rhythm her tooth throbbed—throbbed—throbbed.

Mama got up when she heard Ellen poking around in the pantry, searching for a whole clove to put in her tooth. She lit the lamp. "I was afraid you'd get a toothache, but I didn't have the heart to tell you not to eat that candy. Wish I had now. Come here by the lamp." She fit a piece of clove into the cavity, talking all the while. "Someday we won't have to suffer like this. They say nowadays dentists in big cities put fillings in teeth so they don't have to be pulled. Want to sit and talk awhile?"

Ellen nodded, held her throbbing jaw and sat down on the oven door.

"Might as well knit a few rounds," Mama said, pulling the rocker close to the lamp. "Don't feel very sleepy right now."

"Does a person ever get used to pain?" Ellen mumbled, opening her mouth as little as possible.

"Don't know if we get used to it exactly, but we can take it better if we have a lot. After a big pain little ones don't seem to bother as much. Any better yet?"

Ellen shook her head and Mama's brow furrowed. She rocked gently a little while and said, "Think one of the worst times I had putting up with pain was the time the cow kicked me. I ever tell you about that?"

Ellen shook her head.

Mama cleared her throat like she planned to do a lot of talking. "Let's see . . . it was the winter George was a little over a year old, Al was five—that would make Fred three and you a little over two. Papa was working in the woods that winter in the logging camp and he came home only weekends. Walked home from Ogema Saturday evenings and walked back again Sunday night. Don't know how he did it, but then I don't know how I ever managed those years, either." She stopped rocking and pressed her knitting needle against her lower lip, making a white spot. It was like she was traveling way, way back and it took a little time to get there. Suddenly she began to rock and knit again and words came.

"It was just too much to try to do the milking, and feed and water the stock, and carry wood and water, and shovel snow—and still see that you little ones were taken care of."

Ellen tried not to groan with pain and wished Mama would get on with her story.

"Well, anyway, it was Thursday night, I think. Yes, it was Thursday night and I went out to milk. Just had old Cora left—mean old thing, she was. Milked good though, so we kept her. Well, she wouldn't move over so I swatted her one, and she let loose and kicked me just when I was sitting down to milk her. Caught me on the thigh—bruise as big around as a tea cup—but that wasn't the worst part. I went sailing and hit the end of my spine on the edge of the gutter. Thought my back was broke. Couldn't move my legs at all for a little while. Scared! Oh, my goodness! Here I was out in the barn and couldn't move, and you little ones were all alone in the house. The chance that someone would come by was almost nil. Well, I managed to get up after a few panicky moments, and I bawled some and hollered at that old cow." She chuckled. "As though that would help. I remember crawling to the house over that bumpy, icy path, settin' the milk pail ahead of me, crawling up to it, settin' it ahead of me again until I finally made it to the house. Don't know how I got you little ones to bed, but I know I kept telling myself I'd be better by morning. Well, I wasn't! Not one bit. I bawled all the while I was in the barn so I'd get all cried out and not cry in front of you little ones." She stopped for breath and looked searchingly at Ellen.

"It's a little better," Ellen lied. "How long was it before Papa came home?"

"Well, it happened Thursday night and I knew your Papa wouldn't be home 'til Saturday evening, but I sure did hope Grandpa Verleger or one of the Gebers might come by," she continued, ignoring Ellen's question. "Nearly looked my eyes out up that road, but I decided I'd better not count on anyone coming. Thought about sending Al up to Grandpa's, but it was so bitter cold and the snow was so deep I didn't dare."

She stopped rocking, leaned her head back and closed her eyes, but she kept talking. "Watering the stock wasn't easy, even when I felt well. Had to let a bucket down on a rope into the hole we kept chopped open in the river ice. Had to pull it up and then push it under the fence to the cows. Had to kneel down on the ice and do that over and over 'til they had enough. Had to get water way up to the barn for the sheep and chickens, too. Set the bucket ahead of me and crawled like I did with the milk pail." She opened her eyes and rubbed her knee. "Poor knees really got it. No matter how many rags I wrapped around them I always got cut on the ice. I limped around from chair to chair in the house, but I simply couldn't walk outside and carry a pail."

Hand cupped over her painful jaw, Ellen closed her eyes and tried to imagine Mama's pain and struggle. It didn't ease her pain one bit. It throbbed so badly she wanted to cry. I know what you're trying to do, Mama, she thought, but it just doesn't help.

As though Mama had read her thoughts she said—with a wry laugh, "I know it ain't helping your toothache one bit, but at least you're thinking of something else and the time is going by. Pretty soon your toothache will be gone."

Ellen tried to smile.

Mama took a deep breath and rocked faster. "I got

around a little better by Saturday and went out to feed the stock at noon—my heart in my throat the way it always was when I left you little ones alone. I was almost back to the house when I heard Al and Fred hollering. I hurried in. Couldn't see right away after coming in out of the glaring sun on the snow, but I could make out Al and Fred both standing on a chair by the corner shelf. By the time I got across the room I could see. *Ach, mein Gott!* Fred had Papa's straight-edge razor open in his hand," she demonstrated with a knitting needle. "And Al was trying to pull it away from him. 'Al! Let go!' I yelled and, thank the Lord, he minded. Fred let go too, and the razor clattered to the floor." Mama's knitting needle fell in her lap and she let her head rest on the back of the chair, her body limp as an empty grain sack. "Must have shook for an hour. You know how sharp your papa's straight-edge razor is. I was so riled up I thought I'd just fly into pieces. How was I s'posed to keep you children safe and still do the work? Couldn't take you all with me every time or I'd never get done—much less keep you safe out there. Seemed like I had to put the blame on someone, so I settled on your papa." She looked down at her knitting lying in her lap and spoke softly, like she was talking more to herself than to Ellen. "So stupid. Papa had to work in camp. We had to have money for flour and sugar and salt and kerosene and things. . . ." She looked up at Ellen and said in a confidential tone, "I learned one thing. Love and hate travel side by side. First one's out ahead and then the other. Used to feel awfully guilty when I felt hateful and angry at someone, but I don't anymore. It's natural to feel hate for people at times—especially the ones close to you. I figure we can't help our feelings so I don't worry about them, but giving in to those feelings is wrong—you know, not getting a hold on your feelings and hurting people by saying mean things or doing something spiteful. What I'm trying to say is—we can't help what we feel—but we *can* help what we do."

Mama was still talking, but Ellen wasn't listening. She had to think over what Mama'd just said so she wouldn't forget.

Love and hate travel together . . . natural to hate even the people you love . . . not how you feel that counts— it's what you *do*! She felt light and free. She wanted to yell, "I don't have to feel guilty when I get angry at Mama! I'm not the only one who feels hateful. It isn't only me!"

"Ella?" Mama was saying. "I asked you, care for some warm tea?"

She shook her head. No sense giving that tooth any aggravation. "What happened when Papa got home?"

"Well, he came home a little early that Saturday—found me in bed." Even now Mama looked embarrassed at being found in bed during the day. "I didn't want him to feel sorry for me as much as I wanted him to be proud of me. I wanted to be looking spry when he came. Well, he didn't seem a bit concerned. I was real hurt, I was. He piled into the work though, tired as he was, that I have to say. Sunday morning he took Al out to the barn when he did chores, and pretty soon Al came in pouting 'cause Papa wouldn't take him along to Grandpa's. Said he'd walk too slow. Then I really felt hurt! I didn't care if I cooked dinner or not. Here he was home such a little while and he goes traipsing off to Grandpa's. Wasn't that he had to take care of Grandpa or anything—he didn't usually go running over there.

"In about an hour and a half he came back—all excited. 'Sit down, Emma!' he said. I was in no mood to sit down and listen but I did. 'Emma,' he said. 'How'd you like to board the teacher?' I was dumbfounded. I'd met Jenny Clark a couple times. Took to her right off. But she boarded at Grandpa's right next to the school so she didn't have to walk far in cold weather. Well, your papa went on jabbering like a woman. Seems Jenny didn't get along with Grandpa no-how and wouldn't mind the walk from here— wouldn't even mind sleeping in the cold little room up in the loft. My thoughts were just swarmin'. My goodness! There'd be someone with you children when I went to do chores—except at noon, and someone to talk to evenings. Oh dear, I used to get lonesome after you children were in bed. Couldn't stand hearing all of you all day, but couldn't stand the quiet, either. And a *teacher!* I'd be able to learn so much from her and we sure could use that two dollars a month board."

Mama's eyes sparkled as though she were living that moment right now. "See how quick a person's feelings can change? I was so ashamed of myself! Here your papa'd been thinking and planning how he could fix it so I wouldn't be alone, and I thought he didn't even care. Another thing, I know now he couldn't let me know how sorry he felt for me. He knew I *had* to be strong and face whatever came when I was by myself. One thing I want you to remember: your papa was never, never mean."

"How did you ever get through those years? When you got married did you even *dream* you'd have hard times like that?"

"Well . . . no. I guess not. But a lot of good dreams have come true in my lifetime."

"Good dreams? Like what?"

Mama smiled at Ellen with a faraway look in her eyes. "Having a daughter to sit and talk with like this. That whole day when I was having you, I kept hoping and wishing for a little girl. Between the pains I'd try to picture her—but in all my fancies I never pictured a baby as pretty as you were. Seemed too good to be true the first time I held you. A girl. A daughter to talk woman talk to in a few years. And such a beautiful baby—dark hair and

214

tiny ears. And when you got a little older you had rosy cheeks and your hair fell into ringlets whenever you got warm. Had a hard time punishing you, I did. There were times you should have had a good spanking, and you'd look up at me through those long, dark lashes, and it was like something held my hand back. And your papa was no help. He thought the sun rose and set on you. So when you got a little older, I made up my mind I had to be strict or you'd grow up to be a no-good hussy. Think you can sleep now?" Mama said abruptly to hide the embarrassment of divulging her deep feelings.

Ellen nodded, not daring to look at her. It was like bells ringing and lights flashing—she *had* been born to Mama. Really and truly!

Mama glanced at the clock and shot Ellen a mischievous smile. "Let's get to bed before your papa wakes up. Just look at that clock; we should have been in bed hours ago." She blew out the lamp and they collided in the dark, giggling like schoolgirls. They held each other close for a moment, and Mama whispered, "You'll sleep now," and kissed her forehead.

But the incessant throbbing pain persisted in spite of the carefully inserted clove. Sometimes a piece of clove helped. Not tonight. For awhile she basked in the joy of knowing she was really a Verleger, that Mama had really wanted her, but the pain throbbed on. "Think of pleasant things," she told herself. Mayflowers—clumps of them all over. Pale lavender like the ones she'd picked down by the old house—pure white ones, pink ones. Spring beauties like a pink carpet all around the stone piles. Ugh! Stones. Part of spring, though. Horses plodding up and down the fields, and everyone except the baby and Mama following behind or beside the stone boat, throwing small rocks on it, or stopping to roll on the big ones until the horses strained and the load was dumped on the ever-growing piles.

"Where do they all come from?" she'd asked Papa. Every spring they picked and picked until there wasn't one stone in sight, and next spring—there they were popping up all over the fields again.

"Frost heaves 'em up," Papa said.

Some year there wouldn't be any more coming up. There just couldn't be more every year. But that year had not yet arrived.

She rolled over and tucked the pillow close to her aching jaw. Have to think of something fun. School. School was fun—especially in spring. The contest to see who could see the first birds—the games outdoors at recess—eating lunch under the maple tree—running in the woods in back of the church. And fishing. Soon as supper dishes and the chores were done, away they'd run to the river. Even if fishing was for boys, now and then they'd let her hold a pole. She even put worms on her hook sometimes. She could just feel the tug on the line— another and another until somebody'd yell, "You got a bite!" As if she didn't know. It felt so pleasant she'd let it get a good hold, let it splash and thresh around awhile 'til the firelight caught the gleaming curve of the frantic fish in the air as it threw itself again and again, flopping out of her grasp and picking up twigs and leaves on its beautiful sleek sides. Horrid to see a fish dirty and dry. She'd slip it on a stick with a branch to hold it on, drop it back into the water and tie it to an alder branch. But even if she didn't catch a fish, it was fun to be with other kids. Sometimes it was just nice to sit on a log and watch the firelight from the bonfire reflected in the black ripples, and listen to the rapids around the bend. Then they'd stumble home in the lantern light, and Mama'd be sitting, waiting for them. "Phew! Wash good. You smell like an old Indian," she'd say. And one of the boys would smart back, "Ever smell an old Indian, Ma?" She'd shake her finger at him and tell

216

him not to get sassy, but she'd be smiling all the time.

Bed would feel like a pile of down those nights, and it didn't matter if her hair smelled like smoke or her hands smelled faintly of fish. She'd still see the black swirling water enlivened with shooting red sparks from the fire, and sleep would come too soon.

If only she could sleep now. Tired. So tired, but still the pain nagged on. The dark water—fish line slicing through it. Fish flopping with a soft thud against the soft earth. The suckers would run soon. They're "spawning," Papa said. The boys would scoop them out with a dip net—bushels of them—while the little ones and the girls romped up and down the river banks in the sunshine. Papa said when the alder leaves are as big as a mouse's ear the suckers run. Each year she'd planned to check the size of the leaves, but each year the excitement made her forget.

She'd never forget the acrid smell of the smoke house. Mama smoked the large parts and pickled the tails and fried many a meal crispy brown, coated with cornmeal. Made her mouth water thinking about those suppers of fried suckers, mashed potatoes with lots of butter, and dandelion greens—always dandelion greens with fried suckers. At the first sign of green, Mama'd be out there covering dandelion plants with carefully stored cardboard boxes. Like magic the plants would double their size in a day or two. She'd cut them out of the ground with her sharp little knife, wash them under the pump and cut off the roots, exposing their milky white hearts. Tossed lightly with heavy cream, a dash of vinegar, and sprinkled with sugar, their crisp texture and tangy flavor was tantalizing after the winter's pale, soft foods.

Her stomach rumbled. She shoved a fold of quilt tight against it. There'd be no eating until this pain was gone—a long while gone! She stifled a groan and rummaged through her mind for more pleasant thoughts, like

Mama rummaged through the rag bag for just the right piece of cloth.

A vision of spring struck her fancy. Glorious mountainous thunderheads, fat fluffy puffs that look incredibly soft. Last spring Minnie had sprawled beside her on the sunny green riverbank and they had watched the clouds. "If I had one wish I'd get up there and feel those clouds," Minnie said. "I'd grab a big armful and bring it home and make a nice soft quilt for my doll, and one for Mama and Papa's bed, and one for our bed, and even for all the boys' beds." Ellen hadn't had the heart to tell her they were only tiny droplets of water. That was typically Minnie; always concerned about someone's comfort.

And Mama would drag out every pillow and quilt and all the coats and hang them on the line in the sun. "If you had your way," Papa'd say, "you'd turn the house inside out like a sock and sun the whole bloomin' thing."

"Might just try that," Mama'd answer with a toss of her head. And the house would smell fresh and clean as all outdoors, and there'd be violets in Mama's toothpick holder 'cause it was just the right size.

Violets. The day before Decoration Day they'd pick bunches and bunches of them, tie them with store string to take to the cemetery, and put them on Grandpa and Grandma Kamin's graves and on Mama's sister Anne's grave. Mama'd sink a glass jar into the soil so the wind wouldn't blow it over, fill it with water from Uncle Dick's well across the road, and put the violets in. Mama, Aunt Clara, Aunt Anne, and all the cousins would get together, a bit shy at first, trying to be solemn during the speeches and the program at the cemetery. Then away they'd go like a flock of snowbirds to Uncle Dick's and on to Uncle Walter's a bit farther down the road.

Hard to think about running and laughing now with this pain. Got to sleep. Got to stop thinking. . . .

Daylight. Minnie gone. Hollow in her pillow cold. Bright shaft of light on the wall. Must be late. What day is it? Tomahawk yesterday. That was Monday. It's Tuesday. Should be in school. Toothache. Oh please, God, don't let it ache anymore. She explored the cavity cautiously with her tongue and encountered the taste of clove. Pain gone now.

What time is it? What's Mama doing down there? Thud. Thud. Thud. Pause. Thud. Thud. Thud. Pause. Kneading bread! Must be after nine. So nice to stretch and cuddle down soft and warm. Mama must have decided to let her sleep. When had she *ever* slept this long? A wave of joy flooded over her when she remembered talking with Mama last night. Mama had wanted her—had really *had* her. And even Mama felt hateful at times, but that didn't matter. It was what a person *did* that counted.

For one blissful moment she felt blameless—at perfect peace with herself and God. But only for a moment. Guilt crashed down on her like snow off a roof. The baby. How could she forget! Wishing was *doing* something, wasn't it? Wishing was more than just a feeling. Wishing something bad would happen had to be as bad as doing it. She rolled over and buried her face in her pillow. A groan began deep within her and she let it roll out into the pillow. Down and around her thoughts swirled into the familiar cycle of self-reproach, beginning with the moment she had realized Mama was going to have another baby, on to the day after day of seething resentment and the hope upon hope that something would happen to it, and on to the day Papa had carried out the box made of bright new wood.

Would she ever know where he'd buried it? Unexplainable, this desire to know where. What good would it do to cry over the little grave? She rolled on her back, fists clenched, jaws rigid. Got to stop thinking about it. I'll lose my mind. No way out. Unless . . . unless I tell Mama.

Confession is good for the soul, they say. Oh, it would be so wonderful to tell Mama—hear Mama say, "Why, you poor child. I *know* you're sorry. I forgive you!" But what if she couldn't make Mama understand how she had felt? What if Mama looked at her with eyes full of hate, remembering those awful days when she'd called for her baby and it wasn't there? She shivered and pulled the quilt over her head. The clock struck ten. I'll get up and go downstairs. I'll feel better when I'm wide awake. I'll be all right. Mama and I will work and talk—just so that tooth doesn't start aching again.

Mama was coming in the door with rugs in her arms when Ellen came downstairs.

"Wondered how long you'd sleep," Mama said, looking fresh and cheerful. "I figured anyone who could sleep through all the racket in the morning must need sleep. Toothache gone?"

"Yes!" Ellen said with an exaggerated sigh.

"Good. Be careful when you eat, now." She centered one braided rug in front of the stove and another by the rocker. "There now. House looks real nice. There's nothing like getting something new—something different to do. Why, I've done half a day's work already because I want to start sewing my dress."

"Which piece are you going to make up?"

Mama smiled. "Don't know yet. They're both so pretty I can't decide."

They burst out laughing—a laugh which obliterated last night's hurt and anger.

"Tell you what," Mama said, looking roguish. "I'll hold them both behind me—one in each hand and you pick one."

Mama *was* in a good mood. Mama didn't usually take time for games.

Ellen pointed to Mama's right hand.

Mama held out the old rose piece with the white flowers on it. "I'm glad. Guess I really did like that one best."

After Ellen had eaten breakfast she helped Mama lay out the material and pattern, with much twisting and turning of the pattern pieces to save as much material as possible for quilt-piecing.

"Mmm, I like the smell of new goods. Reminds me of the store and all the things I saw yesterday." She could see the ladies in their elegant braid-trimmed suits, and suddenly Mama's percale looked flimsy and cheap. If Mama could only have a suit like that. But here was Mama chattering happily, eyes sparkling, cheeks faintly pink with excitement—the picture of happiness. Did those ladies look excited and happy when they got those new suits? Maybe they did, but maybe they even found flaws in them. No matter. She just wished those fine ladies could see how happy Mama was over her percale. But then, Mama's eyes could shine over a great many simple things, and how Ellen loved her when she was happy. Ellen loved Papa, too. Papa, riding those slow, slow miles spinning dreams for his family. Papa looking over a newly plowed field, reaping an early harvest in satisfaction, and last night, the way he had enjoyed the sunset.

"Mama? Do you like sunsets?"

"What a silly question. Of course I like sunsets. Who doesn't?"

"Papa says a person should never miss watching one."

Mama's jaws moved with the rhythm of the scissors 'til she finished cutting out the sleeves. She straightened up and rubbed the small of her back, looking out the window toward the old house. "He's right, I suppose. Maybe a person should just set the supper kettles back on the stove off the hot lids and let supper be a few minutes late and look at those pretty colors." She sighed and kept talking as she cut another piece. "Was always so used to rushing. Get supper. Get dishes done. Get the little ones to bed. Get the milk pails washed and yeast set and some darning or some knitting done. Get to bed so I could get up early and start all over again. For me stopping work to look at a sunset is like telling that river down there to stop flowing for awhile."

For a moment there was only the sound of the scissors against the table and the tick of the clock. Mama began putting the leftover pieces in a neat pile. "Still, I don't say it ain't a good idea. Hope you'll get in the habit of taking more time to enjoy things. Life should get easier. Mine's easier than my mother's was—why, I don't even bother to make soap anymore and now we don't think of walking to Ogema like we used to—and when you grow up you'll have machines to do all sorts of things." She laughed. "Just so people don't get so busy earning money to buy those machines that they still don't have time to look at sunsets! My land! It's going on eleven already. Peel potatoes, will you, Ella? Maybe I can get my skirt put together before dinner."

It was nice to hear the click-click, click-click of the sewing machine and the clung-clunk, clung-clunk of the treadle as Mama whistled bits of "When You and I Were Young." Ellen smiled. Mama's happy, all right. She never whistles when she's angry or upset. Bet anything when she sits and puts up the hem by hand she'll sing:

In a quiet country village
Stands a maple on a hill,
Where I sat with my Jeanetta long ago.
And the stars were shining brightly,
And we heard the whip-poor-will,
And we vowed to love each other evermore.

We would sing love songs together
When the birds had gone to rest.

And we'd listen to the ripple of the rill.
I would fold my arms around her,
Lay her head upon my breast,
As we sat beneath the maple on the hill.

We are growing old and feeble,
But the stars are shining still.
And still we hear the murmur of the rill.
Yes, I'll always love you, darling,
As I did that starry night.
As we sat beneath the maple on the hill.

Made Ellen feel so romantic when Mama sang that song. She liked to think that was why Papa insisted that the road be cut around those maple trees—liked to think he was preserving more than just trees.

"Ella! For goodness' sakes. How long does it take to peel enough potatoes for dinner? Get 'em boiling now. *Schnell!*"

While Mama and the little ones napped after dinner, Ellen took the latest copy of *The Youth's Companion* up to her room. Whew! Stuffy! She opened the window and sat on the floor with her arms folded on the window sill, watching the birds circle and swoop over the rocky pasture—their killdeer, killdeer cries sharp and clear on the wind. She took a deep, slow breath of air laden with the mingled fragrances of warm sun on fast-growing grass and warming leaf mold, and wished this special smell would last all summer. Soon the air would smell of dusty roads and dry hay again. A glint of sun on the river caught her eye and she smiled, visualizing the boys romping across the pasture for a quick swim while Papa took a rest after dinner as he always did in hot weather. How comical they looked loping over the bumpy pasture, undressing as they ran, stumbling and tripping over pants legs 'til white legs disappeared over the river bank. Mama'd shake her head when they came panting back—red faced with heat and dark wet spots seeped through their shirts, and say, "Where on earth do they get all that energy?"

Magazine untouched beside her, Ellen shifted to a more comfortable position, leaned her cheek on her sun-warmed arm and closed her eyes. Sheep joined the killdeer chorus. High-pitched "baa's" of lambs answered an octave lower by the ewes—at times two or three of them bleating at once—each in its own special key. She tried to see them, but they were down the hill by the creek. She closed her eyes again, heard the barn door slam, but ignored it. She didn't ever want to move again. So peaceful and pleasant.

But tingling in her leg told her she'd be sorry if she didn't. Reluctantly she got up, tolerated the pins-and-needles feeling and watched Papa walk across the field toward the cedar swamp. Odd to see Papa without the horses. Back toward her, she couldn't see what he was carrying in his hands but he had a shovel over his shoulder. He disappeared into the swamp and came out into the field and headed toward the old house. He veered a bit to the east. Sun gleamed on the bright object he carried. Goose pimples scooted up her arms and crept up into her hairline at the back of her neck. The sun shone brightly on a box. A box made of bright new wood.

Her legs had no strength. She sank back on the floor, knuckles pressed hard against her mouth, holding back the sobs. *Oh, Papa! You didn't dig through all that snow and frozen ground.* Easy to hide the little box deep in the hay until spring. Through a blur of tears she saw him stop a ways east of the old house and she could see him moving. *Oh, Papa, if you only knew. . . .*

She took refuge in her bed—head far under the quilts to muffle her sobs. Now it seemed like no time at all since she'd sobbed over the flour barrel. Oh, but Mama's all right! Then I thought we'd lose her, too. But plain as yesterday she could hear Mama telling her to bring the baby. Mama, hollow-eyed and weak for days and days. And the day her chin had crumpled when she said she wouldn't need the baby clothes again.

I'll never stop crying. Never!

Have to stop. Mama'll be up. Have to go downstairs. She sat up, rummaged under her pillow for a hankie and blew her nose. Got to tell her today. *Got to tell her.*

By the time Mama got up Ellen had bathed her eyes, combed her hair and was setting up the ironing board. Mama had asked her to finish ironing so she could sew.

Mama came out of her bedroom, ran a comb over her hair and tucked in a stray lock. "Well now," she beamed, "I'll be glad to have that ironing done. Was feeling guilty leaving it go while I sewed."

"It's awful to feel guilty, isn't it?" Ellen began. "I've been feeling terribly . . ."

Mama was already sewing. "How's that?" she yelled over the noise of the machine.

"Nothing important," Ellen yelled back. She groaned. No possibility of telling Mama something important while she was sewing. I'll tell her tomorrow. Somehow, I'll tell her tomorrow.

Tomorrow she'd run and see the little grave. That night in bed she continued her plans. She'd cut through the woods after school—pick some flowers on the way.

It was almost noon the next day when Miss McKinley said, "As soon as all of you finish your sums, we'll take time to hear about Ellen's trip to Tomahawk."

Trip to Tomahawk! It seemed so long ago. Scenes were faint now—like a carelessly erased slate still showing faint images. Panic clutched her. What was there to say? Where was all the excitement she had felt—all the things she had seen? Far away now. No time to revive them now. Nine and eight is seventeen . . . carry the one . . . have to tell them *something* . . . five and six is eleven . . . and the one, that's twelve . . . carry the one . . . what can I tell them?

Haltingly, feigning enthusiasm she told them how pretty the river had looked—how wide it was. They fidgeted and whispered. The big stove at Olehofen's store. Some signs of interest. The music coming from the saloon. George rolled his eyes upward in boredom and slid down in his seat. A lump formed in her throat, making it difficult to talk; tears threatened.

"Thank you, Ellen," Miss McKinley interrupted. "Time for recess."

Ellen could feel Miss McKinley's eyes on her as she went to get her lunch pail. This was the end. The very bottom. She had disappointed Miss McKinley.

Before recess was over Miss McKinley managed to catch a moment alone with Ellen. "What's wrong, my dear?"

Ellen shook her head and made her mouth smile. "Nothing!"

Miss McKinley gave her a searching look, a quick one-arm hug, and went to ring the bell.

The afternoon was endless. The pendulum is moving, she thought, why don't the hands move? She made herself listen, but repeatedly her mind drifted. She'd tell Minnie she had to stay and talk to Miss McKinley, and as soon as Minnie was gone she'd hit for the woods. That glass jar on the pantry shelf in the old house—she'd fill it with river water, sink it in the ground to hold the Mayflowers.

An eternity later she was running through the woods, stooping to grab Mayflowers. No time to even smell them. Mama would wonder where she had been if she got home very late.

Carefully she parted the barbed wire fence. Better not tear her school dress. In the clearing now. The sound of her thudding footsteps echoed in her ears as she reached the old house. The jar. Still there! The grave first—then to the river for water.

She rounded the corner of the old house, lunch pail clinking against the jar. *Mama!* There she was, down on her knees, breaking clods of earth and smoothing the little grave like a flower bed. Ellen stepped back. Too late! Mama waved and beckoned for her to come.

"You knew?" Mama asked, looking questioningly at the flowers and the jar.

Ellen nodded. "Saw Papa from my window yesterday."

"Well . . . might as well help me. Careful of your school dress, now."

Ellen knelt beside Mama on the tender grass and crumbled the soft soil from the clumps of sod and tossed the remaining sod into the bushes nearby.

"Left Fred with the little ones. Papa said I'd probably want to do some work here before the ground got all dry and hard." She worked quietly a moment and Ellen's mind whirled. "Seems like a long while ago now. But time heals everything, they say. Always leaves a scar, though. A person can't carry a baby, plan for it, feel it move and then forget it ever existed."

Ellen's arms felt so weak and trembly, she had to work with her elbows resting on her knees. "Mama. I've got to tell you. . . ."

"I don't feel so bad anymore," Mama interrupted. Mama did that sometimes—like what *she* had to say was more important than anyone else. It made Ellen seethe. But not today. Let Mama talk!

"Don't know what I'd have done without your papa those first weeks after the baby came. I'm awfully ashamed to admit it—but I have to tell you." She turned her face away from Ellen. "I wasn't one bit happy when I knew this baby was coming. I had hoped I'd have a couple years to catch up a little bit. Never got a chance to do half the things I planned to do in the new house—and here we're growing out of it already." She swallowed hard and shook her head. "I thought some awful thoughts those first months 'til I felt life. I felt different then. But in December I didn't feel it anymore." She sat back on her heels, hands clenched in her apron. "Those were terrible weeks—waiting, and waiting. It just hung there—like I was carrying around one of those rocks." She shuddered. "Never imagined I'd get so sick. Somehow I didn't mind suffering so much. It was like I was paying for my awful thoughts and wishes. I never meant. . . ."

Her voice broke and she turned her face away. She got control of herself immediately, like she had important things to say. "Your papa knew something was wrong when I didn't sleep nights. I just lay there calling myself a murderer. Tried to tell him it was my fault—that God must have decided I didn't deserve that baby—and what's more that I don't deserve to have any more! Well. Your papa was *so* angry at me. Never saw him so upset."

Mama smoothed the last spot and they stood up and flexed their knees to get the kinks out of them. Mama's eyes roved over the fields where Papa was plowing. "He said he'd never heard such nonsense. Reminded me that just about everyone we know has had at least one baby stillborn—or had one die shortly after birth. It just happens! I had to agree with that. 'You think God don't know how hard you work—how tired you get and how little money we got to raise this big family and that we need a bigger house already?' he said. 'You mean to tell me God don't know our troubles and how we feel better than we do, and don't He know you never wanted anything but to do better for your family? You mean to tell me God would let that baby die just to punish you?" She wiped her eyes on the corner of her apron and gave a sniff.

"Seems like your papa's always right. He don't get so tangled up in his feelings like I do. Still, it took me quite awhile before all that guilty feeling worked out of me." She looked at Ellen for the first time since she had started speaking. "I had to tell you all this. You're awfully young to hear these things, but in just a few years you'll be having your own family, and I don't ever want you going through feeling guilty about something like I did."

Ellen opened her mouth, but words wouldn't come. She looked at the oval of smooth earth and simply nodded.

"Run along, get some water for your flowers," Mama said softly.

She ran down the hill and sobs came out like bubbles out of an uncorked bottle. "Oh, Mama! I never dreamed . . . I didn't know. . . ." It would take awhile for Mama's words to sink in—for her to match Mama's feelings with her own, but it was like cool balm poured on a stinging wound to think of Papa's words.

"Hurry up! Papa's done plowing," Mama yelled.

She gave her eyes a quick splash and wiped them on her sleeve and ran back up the hill.

"My goodness, I didn't plan to be gone this long. We'll have to hurry like the dickens!" She helped Ellen set the jar firmly down into the soil, gave her hands a quick brush on the grass and smiled. "There! Don't they look pretty?" She wheeled around and hiked off across the field.

Ellen picked up her lunch pail and followed. She'd think about what Mama had said, remember every word, and the bad feelings would go away in time—just as Mama's had. She slowed her pace deliberately, letting Mama get ahead of her so she could think and watched the wind whip Mama's apron strings—and she didn't feel one bit like glaring at Mama's back.

The Wonderful World of The Picture Bible

Easiest way imaginable to read the Bible—all the drama and excitement unfold vividly in black-and-white picture strips, easy-to-read dialogue, and captions. All illustrations and statements authenticated by Bible scholars for biblical and cultural accuracy. Enjoy reading these 6 volumes.

OLD TESTAMENT

Creation: From "In the beginning" to the flight from Egypt

The Promised Land: Moses, Ten Commandments, Jericho

Kings and Prophets. David slays Goliath, Solomon displays God's gift of wisdom . . . Elijah's ministry.

The Captivity: Divided kingdom falls . . . Israel is taken into captivity . . . prophecies of a coming Messiah

NEW TESTAMENT

Jesus: The Life of our Lord—His birth, ministry, first followers, crucifixion, and triumph over death

The Church: Angels announce Jesus will return . . . Pentecost . . . Stephen is stoned . . . Paul's conversion, missionary ministry, and death . . . the end of an era.

82701—All 6 books in slipcase. Set, $6.95

Handy order form on last page